Dramascripts

Homer's Odyssey

Adapted by
David Calcutt

Nelson

Thomas Nelson & Sons Ltd
Nelson House
Mayfield Road
Walton-on-Thames
Surrey KT12 5PL
United Kingdom

Designed and produced by Bender Richardson White
Typesetting by Malcolm Smythe
Cover illustration by Dave Grimwood
Black and white illustrations by John James
Printed by L. Rex Printing Co. Ltd., China

This play was commissioned for and first performed by the pupils of Marlborough College in
February 1998, when it was directed by the Head of Drama, Nigel Bryant.

This edition published by Thomas Nelson & Sons Ltd 1999
ISBN 0–17 432562–2
9   8   7   6   5   4   3   2   1
03   02   01   00   99

CONTENTS

SERIES EDITOR'S INTRODUCTION

Dramascripts is an exciting series of plays especially chosen for students in the lower and middle years of secondary school. The titles range from the best in modern writing to adaptations of classic texts such as *A Christmas Carol* and *Silas Marner.*

Dramascripts can be read or acted purely for the enjoyment and stimulation that they provide; however, each play in the series also offers all the support that pupils need in working with the text in the classroom:

- **Introduction** – this offers important background information and explains something about the ways in which the play came to be written.
- **Script** – this is clearly set out in ways that make the play easy to handle in the classroom.
- **Notes** explain references that pupils might not understand, and language points that are not obvious.
- **Activities** – at the end of scenes, acts or sections – give pupils the opportunity to explore the play more fully. Types of activity include: discussion, writing, hot-seating, improvisation, acting, freeze-framing, story-boarding and artwork.
- **Looking Back at the Play** – this section has further activities for more extended work on the play as a whole with emphasis on characters, plots, themes and language.

THE STORY
OF THE *ODYSSEY*

'Odyssey' derives from the Greek word, *Odusseia* which means *The story of Odysseus*. Odysseus was King of the small island of Ithaka, and one of those who fought at, and destroyed, the city of Troy. The *Odyssey* is the story of his journey home, the adventures he had on that journey, and of the final danger he faced upon reaching his kingdom again. But his story cannot properly be understood without also knowing the story of the war at Troy, part of which is told in the *Iliad* – which means *The story of Ilios*. Ilios was another name for Troy. As briefly as possible, then, this is the story behind these two works.

Paris, son of King Priam of Troy, was promised by the goddess Aphrodite, the most beautiful woman in the world, to be his wife. This was Helen, wife of King Menelaos of Sparta, a city on the Greek mainland. Paris went to Sparta, outwardly to visit Menelaos, but secretly to win Helen. This he did, and, while Menelaos was away one time, the two set sail in Paris's ship for Troy. When Menelaos returned and discovered what had happened, he went to his brother, Agamemnon, King of Mycenae, and asked for his help. As the most powerful of the Greek kings, Agamemnon called on all the other kings and heroes of Greece to join him and Menelaos in an expedition against Troy. As all the kings had formerly sworn a pact to assist each other, none could refuse, and the greatest force the world had yet seen assembled at the port of Aulis to sail for Troy. The crossing was made, and Troy was attacked. But it was so well-defended that the Greeks could not break in. So they made camp on the beach below Troy, and a siege began. This siege lasted for 10 years, during which time several battles were fought, but it was only by a trick that the Greeks finally entered Troy. Odysseus devised the plan of building a great wooden horse with a hollow belly. Inside this, a small force of Greeks were hidden. The rest of the force sailed away.

Thinking their enemies had finally given up the siege, and left the wooden horse as an offering to Poseidon, the god of the sea (the horse was one of his creatures), the Trojans opened the gates, took the wooden horse inside, and began to celebrate. But, after the celebrations, and while the Trojans slept, the Greek force, which had only sailed just beyond the horizon, returned. Those inside the wooden horse climbed out, opened the gates, and let the Greek army in. The inhabitants of Troy were massacred, and the city burned to the ground. But, during the 10 years of war, many of the greatest of the Greek heroes, such as Achilles and Ajax, had been killed, and those that survived either met death on the return journey, or were murdered when they arrived home; Agamemnon died in this way.

Odysseus too met hardship on his return journey. Shortly after setting sail from Troy, he incurred the anger of Poseidon, who then vowed to do all he could to prevent the king from reaching his home. For 10 years Odysseus wandered the ocean, enduring storms, and shipwrecks, as well as facing many supernatural dangers. In an attempt to find out how he might finally return home, he was forced to consult the spirit of the blind prophet Tiresias in the land of the dead. Finally, his one remaining ship destroyed, and all his crew drowned, he was kept prisoner on the island of Ogygia by the enchantress Calypso. During this time, the people of Ithaka came to believe he was dead, and many suitors gathered at his palace to bid for the hand of Odysseus's queen, Penelope. She kept them at bay for three years, refusing to give up hope that one day her husband would return. Their son Telemakhos, now grown to manhood, also longed for his father to come back, and restore order to his kingdom. But when Odysseus finally did manage to escape from Calypso and return, in secret, and learned the situation from Telemakhos, he realised he must use trickery to win his kingdom back. Disguising himself as a beggar, he entered his own house to suffer the insults of the suitors while he planned his revenge. Under instructions from his father, Telemakhos advised Penelope to hold a contest to see who she should choose for her husband – this contest being to see which man could string and draw Odysseus's great bow. All that tried failed. Then Odysseus himself, still disguised as a beggar, took up the bow, and strung it. This was the moment when he revealed himself and, with the help of Telemakhos and a few faithful servants, killed all the suitors. So, with Odysseus reunited with his wife and son, order restored to Ithaka, and a long life promised, (though with further wanderings hinted at) the story of Odysseus ends.

THE *ODYSSEY* AND THE *ILIAD*

The *Odyssey* was probably first written down in Ancient Greece around the 8th Century BC, by a poet we have come to know as Homer, who also wrote the *Iliad*. These two, long, epic poems tell the story of the Greek War against the city of Troy, its eventual destruction, and the fates of the surviving Greeks. However, although written down around 2,700 years ago, the stories, legends, and myths that make up these two great poems had been told by travelling storytellers, for about 400 years before that – from the time of the actual Trojan War itself, which has been dated at around 1200 BC. These stories would have been learned by heart and passed on from storyteller to storyteller, with each storyteller maybe adding a little to each story here and there – inserting a new episode, embellishing a description

– so that, as the years passed, the stories grew in length and number.

The language they were told in was the language of verse, not prose, because verse, with its lines of regular rhythm and beat, is easier to memorise than irregular prose.

Homer himself was most likely one of these wandering storytellers or bards, travelling from island to island across the Aegean Sea, walking the roads of the Ancient Greek mainland, going from town to town, city to city telling his tales at festivals or at the firesides of kings. But he had a tool at his disposal that none of the storytellers before him had possessed: that was the skill of writing. At some point in his life, this travelling storyteller – about whom we know nothing except his name – decided to take the various stories he'd been telling, stories which he had learned from other storytellers, to shape them into two massive epic tales, and to fix those epic tales forever in written words. It's in that form that these two books have come down to us today.

What's incredible is not just that these two works have survived for so long, but that they have had such an influence on art, literature and thought, from ancient to modern times. These two works are not only among some of the earliest works written down, they are also among the greatest. Modern translations, children's versions, works of poetry and prose based directly or indirectly on these two works, continue to be written. For them to have endured for so long, for them to have influenced so many writers and artists and musicians over the centuries, for them still to thrill and excite and move us, they must contain some universal, unchanging truth about the nature of human beings – and that is one definition of greatness.

FACT OR FICTION?

Until the end of the 19th Century, it was thought that the stories of the *Iliad* and the *Odyssey* were myth, and had no basis in historical truth. Then, in the 1870s, an amateur German archaeologist named Heinrich Schliemann, driven by a desire to prove the stories true, excavated a hill on the coast of Turkey in the area where tradition said that Troy had stood. There, he discovered the remains of an ancient, and wealthy city that had stood on the site for thousands of years and that, at least twice in its history, had been destroyed by war. He went on to excavate ancient sites on the mainland of Greece and, largely through his pioneering work, the idea that Homer's epic poems did in fact have a basis in an historical event which took place around the year 1200 BC became accepted. Research is still being carried out, and ideas continue to be revised.

What probably happened is something like this: a combined force of warriors drawn from the major city kingdoms from the mainland and islands of what we now call Greece set out to destroy the power of a major Eastern city, called Ilios, or Troy. After a long and drawn-out siege, the city was destroyed. But the war drained the resources of the mainland cities to such an extent that, in their subsequent weakness, they were prone to attack from invading tribes, and were themselves, in their turn, destroyed. The civilisation that had existed on the mainland crumbled, and Greece was plunged into a Dark Age about which we know very little, emerging only into light, and history, again, 400 years later – around the time that Homer composed his epic poems. Sadly, this story of war, and of the disastrous effects it has on civilisation, is only too familiar to us today.

THE GREEK GODS

The Ancient Greeks worshipped a large number of gods and goddesses. Each town, city and village had its own particular deity, that it revered above all others, and each river, spring and tree its own protecting spirit. For the Ancient Greeks, in fact, the whole world was teeming with divine and semi-divine beings, who had to be honoured and placated. These beings could either bring great benefits to their favourites, or wreak terrible destruction on those who had angered them. Many Greek myths are tales of what happened when a human being found favour with a particular god or goddess, or incurred their wrath.

It was Homer, and a contemporary poet of his named Hesiod, who first took this bewildering and confusing array of divine beings, settled on them the names and titles by which we now know them, and ordered the many tales about them into a coherent myth. While it's not necessary to know this myth in order to enjoy the *Odyssey*, some background information on the divinities and supernatural beings who appear in this play might prove useful and informative.

APOLLO
Zeus's son by the goddess Leto. He was one of a pair of twins, the other being his sister, Artemis, goddess of wild things, and the hunt. He was the god, among other things, of poetry and prophecy.

ZEUS
The king of the gods. He overthrew his father, Kronos, after a bitter war, and established himself as ruler of heaven.

HERA
Zeus's sister, and his wife. Along with Zeus, she ruled heaven, and played a large part in directing the affairs of men and women on earth.

ATHENA
Zeus's daughter by the Titan Metis. Unlike other goddesses, Athena did not marry, and was honoured for her wisdom, her judgement, and also for her ferocity in battle. She became the special goddess of the city of Athens, which took its name from her.

HERMES
Son of Zeus and the nymph Maia. He was the gods' messenger to mortals on earth, and also responsible for summoning men and women to their deaths.

POSEIDON
One of Zeus's brothers. He ruled the oceans, and was often called 'Earth-shaker' because of the power he could summon from the waves.

THE *ODYSSEY*

THIS PLAY

This dramatisation of Homer's *Odyssey* is not intended to be a full account of the whole of that great epic poem. No play could be. Nor is it a slavishly faithful one. The demands of creating a piece of theatre are different to those of creating a story, in whatever form it is told or written. With this particular story, dealing in large part as it does with the world of myth and magic, there was a very particular question to be asked at the outset: how, in practical, theatrical terms, can you depict that ancient, archaic world of myth and magic on the stage, and make it real, and comprehensible to a contemporary audience? The answer seemed to be to conceive of the piece as the thing it was – a piece of theatre performed by actors, with limited use of props and costumes, and not to pretend it was anything other than that. Hence the overall structure of the play, which is not Homer's invention but mine, of a band of travelling players performing to an assembled audience of Greeks.

It was an attempt to solve a practical problem, by creating a play within a play, that led to the idea that it was Odysseus himself, in disguise, who had organised this performance of his own wanderings and adventures, as a way of announcing, in secret at first, his return home, prior to revealing himself, and killing those that had overrun his house. When this idea came, it seemed more than apt. For, in Homer, Odysseus, among other things, is depicted throughout as a dissembler and deceiver, a man prone, through the necessity of just trying to survive, to donning disguises, making up stories, pretending he's other than he is. In solving a simple, practical problem, I'd been led to what, for me, is the heart and essence of Homer's poem.

For what the poem is about – the meaning behind that hazardous voyage through a world populated by gods, goddesses, witches and monsters – is the attempt by a man to defy fate, to kick free of the chains of superstition and destiny that bind him, and take control of his own life and his own world. This is the central drama of the play, and this, I believe, is what makes Odysseus not only the first truly human hero in literature, but an enduring, and contemporary one. For, whether we call those forces that we feel guiding and shaping our lives gods, or destiny, or evolution, we all of us understand,

and share, Odysseus's rage against them, his desire to defy them, and shape his own future. To what extent he succeeds or fails – and to what extent we succeed or fail – is the human heart of this timeless story.

This play was commissioned by, and first produced at, Marlborough College, in February 1998, and directed by Nigel Bryant. In that production there was no set. The acting space consisted of a semi-circular sanded floor. This empty space was left free to become all the locations of the play – from Odysseus's palace to the Cyclops' cave to the Land of the Dead, without there being any need to interrupt the flow of action with changes of set or scenery. Given the importance of this fluidity of action, this seemed to me to be the ideal way of staging the play.

THE CHARACTERS

(The pronunciation of the names is also given.)

At Odysseus's Palace

EURYKLEIA	(**YOO**-RI-*KLEYE*-A)	*slave, nurse to Odysseus in his childhood*
EUMAIOS	(**YOO**-*MAY*-OS)	*slave*
MELANTHIOS	(**MEL**-*AN*-THI-OS)	*slave*
TELEMAKHOS	(**TEL**-*EM*-AK-OS)	*Odysseus's son*
ANTINOÖS	(**AN**-TIN-*O*-OS)	
EURYDAMAS	(**YOO**-RI-*DAM*-AS)	
AMPHIMEDON	(**AM**-FI-*MEE*-DON)	
EURYMAKHOS	(**YOO**-*RI*-MAK-OS)	*suitors*
LEOKRITOS	(**LAY**-*OK*-RIT-OS)	
LEODES	(**LAY**-*O*-DEEZ)	
PENELOPE	(**PE**-*NE*-LOP-EE)	*Odysseus's wife*
SLAVES		

The Players who act out the *Odyssey*.

NOMAN

SAILORS

POLYPHEMOS (PO-LI-*FEE*-MOS)

CYCLOPS (*SEYE*-KLOPS)

EURYLOKHOS (YOO-*RI*-LOK-OS)

MAIDENS: LION, WOLF, BOAR, FOX, LEOPARD, BEAR

CIRCE (*SIR*-SEE)

HERMES (*HUR*-MEEZ) *the gods' messenger, Zeus's son*

TIRESIAS (TEYE-*REE*-SEE-AS)

TIRESIA (TEYE-*REE*-SEE-A)

LEUKOSIA (LOO-KO-*SEE*-A)

AGLAOPE (AG-*LAY*-O-PAY)

KHARYBDIS (KA-*RIB*-DIS)   } *sirens*

SKYLLA (*SKI*-LA)

ZEUS (ZYOOS) *the king of gods*

HERA (*HEE*-RA) *Zeus's sister and wife*

POSEIDON (PO-*SEYE*-DON) *god of the oceans, Zeus's son*

GHOST-FIGURE

ATHENA (ATH-*EE*-NA) *a goddess, Zeus's daughter*

APOLLO (A-*POL*-OH) *god of poetry and prophecy, Zeus's son*

THE ODYSSEY
SCENE 1
How The Players Arrived at Ithaka

The hall in ODYSSEUS'S palace on Ithaka. EURYKLEIA and other SLAVES enter. *They are setting out the hall for a feast. One of them carries a chair and places it, central. EURYKLEIA is in charge, and giving the others their orders. There's a sense of haste and urgency about the whole operation.*

EURYKLEIA   Hurry! They'll be arriving soon. And if everything's not   1
ready when they do, it'll be our backs that'll pay for it.
(She turns and speaks to the audience.) It's a sad day. Here we
are, preparing for a wedding feast, yet my heart feels like
breaking. It's a funeral feast, more like, for my master . . .
Odysseus, king of Ithaka. Or so he was, until he went away
to fight at Troy. Went away, and never came back. Drowned
at sea, no doubt, or murdered by pirates or barbarians. It
makes no difference. He's gone, and we'll never see him

Ithaka *An island off the western coast of Greece, in the Ionian Sea. The nearby island of Kefalonia, Zakynthos and Lefkas would also probably have been part of Odysseus's kingdom*

and other slaves *Slavery was practised by most cultures of the ancient world. Slaves were usually prisoners taken in war, or from raids on other towns or cities.*

until he went away to fight at Troy *See* The Story of Odysseus.

or barbarians *This word derives from a Greek term for anyone who could not speak Greek, and whose language sounded like bar-bar-bar. In other words, anyone who was not civilised.*

---

again. I was his nurse. It was me who raised him, from $\qquad$ 10
childhood to manhood. Good days, they were. But the
good days are gone, and it breaks my heart to see his
kingdom as it is now. There are plenty more who feel like
me, but these days, on Ithaka, we're not allowed to show it.

*During the above, EUMAIOS has entered, struggling with a large
and heavy chair. EURYKLEIA turns to him.*

EURYKLEIA   What's going on? That's Odysseus's chair!

EUMAIOS   Is it? It's heavy enough . . .

EURYKLEIA   What are you doing with it . . . and who are you?

EUMAIOS   My name's Eumaios.   20

EURYKLEIA   Eumaios . . . ?

EUMAIOS   I'm a swineherd. I look after pigs . . .

EURYKLEIA   I know what a swineherd is. But what's a swineherd doing
with the master's chair?

MELANTHIOS enters.

MELANTHIOS   Take that out!

EUMAIOS   But I was told to bring it in . . .

MELANTHIOS   I don't care what anybody said! I'm telling you to take it,
and yourself, out!   30

EUMAIOS suddenly recognises MELANTHIOS.

EUMAIOS   Melanthios! The goat-herd. *(He puts down the chair, walks
closer to MELANTHIOS.)* I didn't recognise you in those fine
clothes.

I'm a swineherd *In the days when a great part of a family's wealth was
calculated from the number of herds of animals he owned, the keeper of
these animals, even though a slave, was a person of some standing. Homer
recognises this by giving Eumaios the swineherd a key role in his Odyssey.*

MELANTHIOS	I'm not a goat-herd anymore . . .
EUMAIOS	(He sniffs.) It's a hard smell to get rid of . . .
MELANTHIOS	I have a high position here . . .
EUMAIOS	(Holds his nose.) You're high, all right . . .
MELANTHIOS	(He grabs hold of EUMAIOS, threatening him.) If you're not careful, it won't just be the pigs we'll be sticking for the feast!
	He pushes EUMAIOS away. EUMAIOS stumbles into and over the chair.
EUMAIOS	You wouldn't have done that if Odysseus was here . . . !
MELANTHIOS	But he's not, is he? Now get yourself, and that chair, out!
EUMAIOS	Not until the man who ordered me to bring it in tells me otherwise.
MELANTHIOS	And who might that be?
EUMAIOS	A better man than any of us here. My master's son. Telemakhos.
MELANTHIOS	(Stiffening a little, and backing off.) Indeed? The royal orphan has pig-keepers for company these days, does he?
EUMAIOS	I've known him since he was a boy, and I've served his father, and his father's father, since I was a boy myself.
MELANTHIOS	Well, then. Let it stay, for now. Let Telemakhos have his way . . . while he still can. But if you're wise, old man, you'll be looking to serve a new master before this day's out!
	MELANTHIOS goes. EURYKLEIA turns to the other slaves, who have been watching.
EURYKLEIA	What are you standing about for? There's a feast to be prepared. Get on with your work! (The slaves continue preparing the feast. EURYKLEIA turns to EUMAIOS.) I hate that

40

50

60

	man. What is he? A slave, like you and me. But he swaggers around the place like a prince.	
EUMAIOS	What was that he meant about a new master?	
EURYKLEIA	Didn't Telemakhos tell you?	
EUMAIOS	He told me there was to be a feast, and to bring this chair in. But that's about all.	
EURYKLEIA	You don't know, then?	70
EUMAIOS	Know what?	
EURYKLEIA	He probably couldn't bring himself to tell you.	
EUMAIOS	Tell me what?	
EURYKLEIA	Too ashamed, I should think.	
EUMAIOS	What are you talking about?	
EURYKLEIA	His mother's getting married.	
EUMAIOS	What?	
EURYKLEIA	This is to be our mistress's wedding-feast. Lady Penelope's going to choose a new husband.	

TELEMAKHOS enters, carrying a bow, a quiver of arrows, and a   **80**
hunting horn.

Lady Penelope's going to choose a new husband *In Ancient Greece, kingship was a male role. A woman was not entitled to rule alone. But a man could become king by virtue of marriage – either to the daughter of the old king, or, as in this case, the wife of one deceased. Kingship certainly was not passed on from father to son, which is why Telemakhos is powerless to get rid of the suitors.*

a bow, a quiver of arrows *Odysseus's bow had been given to him when he was a young man. It was a prized possession, which is why he did not take it with him when he went to fight at Troy, and it was of such power that only Odysseus was able to bend and string it.*

TELEMAKHOS	A new husband for my mother, a new father for me, a new king for Ithaka.
EURYKLEIA	And a bad day for us all.
TELEMAKHOS	For someone it will be a good day. Cause for celebration indeed. *(To EUMAIOS.)* Put my father's chair over there, next to my mother's.

EUMAIOS picks up the chair, struggles with it to place it next to PENELOPE'S chair, speaking as he does.

EUMAIOS	You didn't tell me any of this. Your mother's marrying! Who?
TELEMAKHOS	I don't know. She has a wide choice. Men from all over the kingdom, and beyond. Princes, landowners, merchants. They're all here.

100

EURYKLEIA	And have been for the last three years, drinking, brawling, eating us out of house and home . . .
TELEMAKHOS	Not for much longer. Today the business will be settled once and for all. When my mother chooses one for her husband . . .
EURYKLEIA	Whoever she chooses won't come close to being the man your father was!

I hardly even remember him *Odysseus has been gone from Ithaka for 20 years. The war at Troy ended 10 years ago, and lasted for 10 years before that. Telemakhos was only a small child when his father left home.*

5

TELEMAKHOS	My father? Who is he? A fading memory. A ghost. I hardly even remember him.

110

EUMAIOS	*(With passion.)* He's a man I'll never forget!

TELEMAKHOS looks at EUMAIOS, and smiles.

TELEMAKHOS	I know you won't, Eumaios. And I'm glad of it. *(Lovingly, TELEMAKHOS hangs the arrows, bow and hunting horn from the sides of the chair.)* There. It's ready now. *(He turns to the others.)* Everything's ready.

MELANTHIOS enters.

MELANTHIOS	And not before time. Telemakhos . . . your guests are here.

The SUITORS, led by ANTINOÖS, enter in grand manner, chatting, laughing. TELEMAKHOS sits in his father's chair. ANTINOÖS approaches TELEMAKHOS.

120

ANTINOÖS	Telemakhos. My hand.

He holds out his hand. TELEMAKHOS swings his leg over the arm of the chair

TELEMAKHOS	Antinoös. My foot.
ANTINOÖS	I see you still have your sense of humour. *(TELEMAKHOS stares hard at ANTINOÖS.)* And that chair – your father's I believe – is it some kind of joke?
TELEMAKHOS	My father's chair is no laughing matter.
ANTINOÖS	On the contrary. I find its presence here highly amusing.

130

The other SUITORS laugh at this.

And that chair . . . your father's I believe *This is no ordinary, everyday chair. It is something akin to a throne, and sacred to Odysseus. It is almost as if the spirit of Odysseus lives on within it. By sitting himself in it, Telemakhos is taking on something of the spirit of his father and, as such, offering a challenge to the power of the suitors.*

TELEMAKHOS	As you're all in such a . . . festive mood, let's have some entertainment. Begin as we mean to go on, eh? Eumaios. Give us one of your songs. One to stir the blood, set the heart thumping and the spirit soaring. Give us a song of Troy.
ANTINOÖS	*(Sharply.)* No! *(Softens his tone.)* Please, not that. No songs about Troy, or any of its . . . glorious heroes.
EURYDAMAS	They're hardly in keeping with these happier times.
AMPHIMEDON	All those battles, all that bloodshed.
EURYMAKHOS	All that strutting, and those bellowing voices.
LEOKRITOS	All those hairy men smelling of sweat.
LEODES	Ancient history, dead and gone.
ANTINOÖS	And those that aren't are old men who've lost their wits and their continence.
EUMAIOS	*(Angrily.)* There's a few things old men could still teach these young ones.
ANTINOÖS	What? What did you say?
EUMAIOS	Manners and respect would do for a start.
EURYMAKHOS	I can smell something.
AMPHIMEDON	Pigs. He smells of pigs!
EUMAIOS	At least it's an honest smell.
LEOKRITOS	How dare you!
ANTINOÖS	I'd thought everything was ready for the feast. Obviously it isn't. There's still some filth needs sweeping out. Melanthios. Throw this garbage into the yard where it belongs.
MELANTHIOS	Nothing will give me greater pleasure, my lord Antinoös.
	MELANTHIOS steps forward to take hold of EUMAIOS.

140

150

7

TELEMAKHOS jumps up from his chair.   160

TELEMAKHOS   Leave him! *(MELANTHIOS ignores TELEMAKHOS and takes hold of EUMAIOS. TELEMAKHOS goes across and pulls MELANTHIOS round.)* Leave him, I said!

MELANTHIOS   I only act at my masters' bidding.

TELEMAKHOS strikes MELANTHIOS, knocking him down.

TELEMAKHOS   This man's my guest. I invited him. He stays.

ANTINOÖS   Take care, Telemakhos. I'll only be pushed so far.

TELEMAKHOS   Oh, no. I think I can push you further.

ANTINOÖS   Who do you think you are . . . ?

PENELOPE has entered.   170

PENELOPE   He is his father's son! *(To TELEMAKHOS.)* You wish this slave to stay, Telemakhos?

TELEMAKHOS   I do.

PENELOPE   Then he shall. Does anyone object?

ANTINOÖS   Of course not, Lady Penelope. You are our mistress, and we are all your slaves.

PENELOPE   So. The matter's settled. *(PENELOPE sits. She indicates that TELEMAKHOS should sit also. He does.)* Is everyone assembled?

EURYMAKHOS   We are, my lady, and eager to learn which one of us you've   180
chosen.

EURYDAMAS   Which of us is to have the honour of being named as your husband.

AMPHIMEDON   New father to your gentle son, new protector to the citizens of Ithaka . . .

LEODES   And worthy successor to its former lord, the illustrious, and deceased, Odysseus.

LEOKRITOS	We wait, my lady, upon your word.
PENELOPE	You shall hear it in due course. But for now, please, take your places. My son has arranged some entertainment for us all.

190

The SLAVES show the SUITORS to their places.

ANTINOÖS	What kind of entertainment? A rousing song from our friend here?
TELEMAKHOS	No. It's a play.
EURYDAMAS	A play!
LEODES	I don't know of any actors on Ithaka.
TELEMAKHOS	A band of players arrived here from Scheria last evening.
EURYMAKHOS	Why didn't you inform us of this?
TELEMAKHOS	Forgive me, Eurymakhos. I didn't realise it was necessary . . .

200

PENELOPE	That's enough! There'll be no more arguments!
ANTINOÖS	As always, the Lady Penelope is right. This is a day for sealing friendships and alliances, a day for the healing of old wounds. Let us have your play.
TELEMAKHOS	Eumaios. Go and tell the players they may enter.
EUMAIOS	Yes, my lord.

EUMAIOS goes to the doors and opens them. Immediately, the PLAYERS burst in. All are masked, and they carry with them

No. It's a play *An invention for the purpose of this dramatisation. As far as we can tell, such things as travelling players were unknown at this time. Drama, in fact, as we understand it today, was not created in Greece until the 5th Century BC – 400 years after Homer wrote his epic poems, and 800 years after the time when they, and this play, are set.*

Scheria *Probably present day Corfu.*

9

their props and costumes. The PLAYERS run and leap among all **210**
those gathered in the hall, shouting, calling out, and causing
general havoc and chaos. The SUITORS are bewildered and
outraged. TELEMAKHOS is amused. PENELOPE maintains her
composure. Then, at a signal from one of the PLAYERS, all stop.
There is silence. The PLAYERS turn and speak to their audience.

PLAYERS   Noble Greeks, of high degree,
We bring a story of the sea
And one who sailed it, forced by fate
To wander round the wide world's plate,
Bereft, abandoned, and alone,   **220**
Cursed by the gods, stripped to the bone,
A man without a name or home
Whose only friends were wind and foam.
Break down these walls let ocean pour
In through the doors, let breakers roar!
Let thunder roll! Let lightning crack!
Come salt and spray! Come storm and wrack!
And join us, as, without delay,
We play for you our Noman play.

The SUITORS and SLAVES resume their positions, and the **230**
PLAYERS make ready to perform their play.

HOT-SEATING In small groups, one of you takes on the role of Telemakhos. The others question him to find out how he feels about the suitors taking over his house, the possibility of his mother marrying one of them, and how he feels about his absent father.

ACTING In twos, one of you take on the role of Eumaios, and one that of Eurykleia. Eurykleia believes that Odysseus is dead, whereas Eumaios believes he is not and that one day he will return.

Create a scene in which the two argue over this, each trying to justify their case. Set the scene in a particular time and place, and give the two characters some activity they're involved in while they talk.

DISCUSSION: CHARACTER As a class, discuss how you would best describe the characters of the suitors.

What reasons might they have for thinking Penelope might choose one of them for her husband?

DISCUSSION: WRITING In small groups, discuss how you think Penelope feels about the situation in her house.
- Does she wish to marry again?
- Has she given up all hope of Odysseus's returning?
- Why has she, after three years, finally decided to choose one of them?

After this discussion, write a short monologue by Penelope, giving her thoughts and feelings.

LANGUAGE In this scene, there are two *castes* of characters: the rich, land-owning caste (which includes Odysseus's family, and the suitors), and the slave caste.

As a class, look closely at the way both kinds of characters speak in the scene, and discuss what difference you can find between the kinds of language they use.

ARTWORK In the introduction, it is suggested that there should be no, or little fixed set for the play. If you were directing this scene for the theatre, how would you create the hall of Odysseus's palace?

Think about what props you might use, remembering that most of them would need to be brought on by the actors, and think about where you would position the various characters. Remember that, at the end of the scene, the players enter, and take over the stage for the performance of their play.

Make a sketch showing your ideas, with written notes on it where necessary.

11

Scene 2
The Cyclops

A drumbeat begins, slow and steady. A group of five SAILORS, with NOMAN standing central, face outwards. As the SAILORS speak, they mime and enact some of what they describe. For the time being, NOMAN remains still.

1st SAILOR	Imagine a ship.	1
2nd SAILOR	Imagine a ship on a wide sea.	
3rd SAILOR	Imagine a ship on the world-wide, wine-dark sea.	
4th SAILOR	A big-bellied sail, creak of timber and rigging.	
5th SAILOR	Wind-crack, wave slap, the salt-sting of spray.	
1st SAILOR	Hands gripped to the oars . . .	
2nd SAILOR	Pull . . . ! Lift . . . ! Drop . . . ! Pull . . . !	
3rd SAILOR	Shoulders and back muscles strained to breaking!	
4th SAILOR	Every bone in the body aching!	
5th SAILOR	Every nerve and sinew screaming!	10
1st SAILOR	As we ride the ship over the white-topped water . . .	
2nd SAILOR	Through the whole, deep groaning roll of the ocean.	
3rd SAILOR	Behind us, the sweet incense of war . . .	
4th SAILOR	A city burned, Troy of the shining towers . . .	

 The Cyclops *In Ancient Greek mythology, the Cyclops were a race of primitive, one-eyed giants. It was they who manufactured the thunderbolts with which Zeus defeated his father and the Titans.*

5th SAILOR	Smoked ruins offered to the bloody mouthed god.
1st SAILOR	Ahead of us, an unknown destination . . .
2nd SAILOR	Uncharted territories, earth's mystery map.
3rd SAILOR	Around us, thick night, and a mist filled with moonlight . . .
4th SAILOR	Strange lights on the water, a midnight stillness.
5th SAILOR	And suddenly, there, the sound of breakers!
1st SAILOR	And suddenly, there, rising out of the dark . . .
2nd SAILOR	The hump-backed crag-black lump of an island!
3rd SAILOR	And we take the oars and we guide her in . . .
4th SAILOR	Hull slapping the shallows . . .
5th SAILOR	Keel scraping the gravel . . .
1st SAILOR	Scramble out, drag her safe on to the shore . . .
2nd SAILOR	Then stumble up the beach, find shelter in the rocks . . .

 the bloody mouthed god *They're referring to Ares, god of war. Ares was the son of Zeus and Hera.*

3rd SAILOR	And drop down worn and exhausted among them . . .	40
4th SAILOR	And sleep all night, our dreams rocking . . .	
5th SAILOR	To the night-long, sing-song rhyme of the waves.	

They sleep. NOMAN speaks to the audience.

NOMAN While they slept I heard it. A cry, somewhere above and beyond me, rising up out of the darkness. A wild, inhuman, terrible cry. Like the voice of the monstrous earth itself. It rose, and fell, then rose again, and fell, and rose and fell once more. Three times it sounded, and then it was gone. All night I stood, listening for it, but it never came again.   50

The SAILORS wake and rise.

1st SAILOR Next morning we awake with the sunrise.

2nd SAILOR Stretch our limbs, take stock of the situation.

3rd SAILOR Up from the shore, the ground rises steeply.

4th SAILOR A tree-covered hill, bird-cry and goat-bleat.

5th SAILOR No sign of any human dwelling.

1st SAILOR Just a crag rising black against the sky.

2nd SAILOR And a wide cave gaping from the wall of rock.

The SAILORS now speak to each other and NOMAN.

3rd SAILOR I don't like the place. It makes me uneasy.   60

4th SAILOR Like we're being watched.

5th SAILOR But we're all hungry and thirsty, and supplies are running low.

1st SAILOR There's fresh water here, and I've heard goats bleating.

2nd SAILOR I say we get water and meat, and take ship again.

3rd SAILOR I'm all for that. And the quicker the better.

4th SAILOR	The sooner we leave here, the sooner we'll be home.
5th SAILOR	What do you say, captain? What shall we do?

They all look at NOMAN in anticipation. He considers a while before answering. 70

NOMAN	I think we'll go and take a look around.

The SAILORS narrate and mime.

Ist SAILOR	So we follow him.
2nd SAILOR	Just like we always do.
3rd SAILOR	Climbing upwards, winding through the undergrowth . . .
4th SAILOR	Sweat in our eyes, flies plaguing our faces . . .
5th SAILOR	And somehow as well as climbing upward . . .
Ist SAILOR	It seems we're also climbing backward . . .
2nd SAILOR	Backward into an earlier time . . .

80

3rd SAILOR	A time before men, before gods even . . .
4th SAILOR	The time of the world's first making . . .
5th SAILOR	When ancient, nameless spirits had the whole earth for their home . . .
Ist SAILOR	And this island with its forest is their last refuge on the earth . . .
2nd SAILOR	Where you can almost see them in the gold-black shadows . . .
3rd SAILOR	Almost hear them in the rustle and whisper of the leaves . . .

90

4th SAILOR	Where their bodies are these rocks that burst from the bushes . . .
5th SAILOR	Stone heads and stone faces, blind stone eyes and gaping stone mouths . . .

1st SAILOR	And we can feel the hungry magic of the place stirring to life and leading us on . . .
2nd SAILOR	To where the path opens out and the sun glares down . . .
3rd SAILOR	And we stand on a wide ledge halfway up the mountain . . . 100
4th SAILOR	With a cave before us, hung with roots and creepers . . .
5th SAILOR	And the path ends here and there's nowhere else to go.
	The SAILORS gather once more about NOMAN.
1st SAILOR	Well, captain, what now?
2nd SAILOR	Go back down, or go in there?
3rd SAILOR	I don't fancy the place myself.
4th SAILOR	It smells of danger. I say we keep out.
5th SAILOR	You tell us what to do, captain, and we'll jump straight to it.
	Once again, NOMAN considers before answering. 110
NOMAN	We took the trouble to climb up here. It'll do no harm to take a look inside.
	SAILORS narrate.
1st SAILOR	We go in.
2nd SAILOR	It's immense.
3rd SAILOR	A massive stone chamber.
4th SAILOR	Like the inside of some great stomach.
5th SAILOR	The hollowed-out belly of a monstrous whale.
1st SAILOR	And it's not empty.
2nd SAILOR	There's a smell of woodsmoke and goat. 120

3rd SAILOR	Shelves lined with cheeses, a stack of firewood in the corner.
4th SAILOR	Skins filled with water.
5th SAILOR	Barrels full of milk.
lst SAILOR	Someone lives here, all right.
2nd SAILOR	But who? And do we want to meet him?
3rd SAILOR	Me, I'm not sure. I've got this bad feeling.
4th SAILOR	And me. Let's not stay.
5th SAILOR	Just grab some food and go.
lst SAILOR	Get our supplies, go back down the mountain.
2nd SAILOR	Push the ship into the shallows.
3rd SAILOR	Leave this place behind us, head for the open sea.
4th SAILOR	What do you think, captain?
5th SAILOR	How's that for a plan?
NOMAN	Sneaking in and scurrying off like a pack of thieves? We're not bandits, are we? Or pirates? Or barbarians? We're Greeks and we'll stay. And you never know, if we're lucky, it might give us a story to tell the folks back home.
	SAILORS speak to the audience.
lst SAILOR	So we stay.
2nd SAILOR	And we wait.
3rd SAILOR	There in the dark.
	Slow drumbeat begins.
4th SAILOR	Till we hear the sound of goats bleating outside . . .
5th SAILOR	And footsteps on the path, climbing up . . .

130

140

lst SAILOR	Big, heavy, ground-shaking footsteps . . .
2nd SAILOR	And they're getting nearer . . .
3rd SAILOR	And the goats come flocking in . . .
4th SAILOR	And this huge shadow blocks out the light . . . 150
5th SAILOR	And we scatter!

The SAILORS and NOMAN scatter as the drumbeat rises to a crashing crescendo on the entrance of POLYPHEMOS, a terrible, giant creature with a single, red, staring eye in the middle of its head.

lst SAILOR	He stands before us, a monster of a man!
2nd SAILOR	Body thick-coated with matted hair!
3rd SAILOR	And right there in the middle of his face . . .
4th SAILOR	A single eye like a blazing furnace . . .
5th SAILOR	His whole, huge body the hot, hungry oven . . . 160
ALL	That opens the doors of its mouth and . . .
POLYPHEMOS	ROOOOAAAAARRRRR!

POLYPHEMOS grabs two of the sailors and drags them off as other SAILORS narrate.

lst SAILOR	Then this creature grabs two of us . . .
2nd SAILOR	One in each hand . . .
3rd SAILOR	Smashes their brains out against a rock . . .
lst SAILOR	Stuffs them into his mouth, gulps them down . . .
2nd SAILOR	Rolls a great stone across the entrance . . .

  on the entrance of POLYPHEMOS . . . *Polyphemos is a Cyclops.*

3rd SAILOR	And lies down among his goats, and sleeps.	170

Having eaten the two SAILORS, POLYPHEMOS lies down and sleeps. The surviving SAILORS crouch in fear. NOMAN speaks to the audience.

NOMAN   I saw it all. I watched it happen. And though it was terrible, it came as no surprise. When I'd heard those cries the night before, I'd known they were calling us to something like this. As clearly as if the gods had spoken. For they're hostile to us, mean us only harm. When they call, it's to doom and the dark. And when they do, you'd best whistle, and trust in your own hands.   180

The SAILORS gather around NOMAN. They speak to him while he speaks to the audience.

lst SAILOR   Captain!

NOMAN   The mountain-track was our destiny's path.

2nd SAILOR   What shall we do?

NOMAN   This horror that awaited us, our fate's decree.

3rd SAILOR   How can we escape?

NOMAN   And the best a man can do is to go to it grinning.

lst SAILOR   You led us into this.

NOMAN   And maybe find a way of making a name for himself.   190

2nd SAILOR   Now get us out.

NOMAN   Something that will live on after he's gone down to the dark.

3rd SAILOR   Captain! Are you listening?

lst SAILOR   This monster's going to eat us all.

2nd SAILOR   We're fresh meat in his larder.

3rd SAILOR   Breakfast, dinner and supper.

ALL	How are you going to get us out?

NOMAN turns to the sailors.

NOMAN	Don't worry. Leave it to me. I'll think of something. 200

He sits. The SAILORS move away from him, sitting also.

Ist SAILOR	Night comes, and we sit in the dark.
2nd SAILOR	All we can do is pray he comes up with the goods.
3rd SAILOR	Night passes. Morning comes.
Ist SAILOR	The monster wakes, eats two more of us.
2nd SAILOR	Then goes out with the goats and blocks up the entrance.
3rd SAILOR	And still he's just sitting there, and still he says nothing.
NOMAN	I heard nothing. I saw nothing. I was following the crooked path of my thoughts, searching the innermost 210 cave of my mind. A safe place, where the gods couldn't find me. And I sat there, alone, thinking, scheming, trying out one plan after another.

During the above, POLYPHEMOS has risen. He now turns his attention to the SAILORS again, and they scuttle back in fear.

Ist SAILOR	By this time, it's evening, and the monster's back.
2nd SAILOR	Hungry as ever, feasting on us.
3rd SAILOR	Two more men killed.
Ist SAILOR	Torn.
2nd SAILOR	Chewed. 220
3rd SAILOR	Swallowed.
Ist SAILOR	And this cannibal creature's standing there in the cave . . .
2nd SAILOR	Wiping the blood from its mouth . . .

3rd SAILOR	Picking its teeth with a bone . . .
NOMAN	Then the plan came to me, and I knew what to do.
	NOMAN jumps to his feet and approaches POLYPHEMOS.
NOMAN	Hey, you! Round-Eye! Cyclops. What's your name?
POLYPHEMOS	My name? What do you want to know that for?
NOMAN	If I'm going to be eaten by you, you could at least do me the honour of telling me your name
POLYPHEMOS	You're going to be eaten, all right. Eaten by Polyphemos. That's my name.
NOMAN	Well, Polyphemos. Haven't you got anything to wash your meal down with?
POLYPHEMOS	Of course I have. Goat's milk
NOMAN	Goat's milk! Is that all?
POLYPHEMOS	What's wrong with goat's milk?
NOMAN	Nothing. If you haven't got anything better.
POLYPHEMOS	And have you got something better?
NOMAN	It just so happens I have. Wine.
	He unties a skin-bag of wine from his belt and holds it up.
POLYPHEMOS	Wine? What's that? Never heard of it. Is it good to drink?
NOMAN	Why don't you try it? See what you think.
	NOMAN hands the bag of wine to POLYPHEMOS. He drinks from it.

230

240

Round-Eye! Cyclops *The word cyclops derives from the Greek meaning* round eye.

. . . Polyphemos. That's my name *His name comes from two Greek words – poly, meaning* much *or* great, *and phemos meaning* famous. *Therefore his name means something like* greatly famed.

POLYPHEMOS	It's delicious! Wonderful! So smooth and sweet!
	It's nectar from heaven, a tasty treat!
	I've tasted nothing like this before.
	Now it's all gone, and I want some more.	250
	More! More! MOre! MOre! MORE!

NOMAN   Of course. Be my guest. Have as much as you like.

NOMAN passes another wineskin across. POLYPHEMOS drinks again as the SAILORS speak.

1st SAILOR   So the Cyclops drinks some more.

2nd SAILOR   And it goes straight to his head.

3rd SAILOR   And by this time he's staggering about the cave.

1st SAILOR   Flushed and befuddled, and roaring out.

POLYPHEMOS sways from side to side and speaks drunkenly.

POLYPHEMOS   You've made me a gift, now I'll do the same.   260
              All you've got to do is tell me your name.

NOMAN   Certainly. My name's Noman. That's what everybody
          calls me. Noman.

POLYPHEMOS   Noman, here's my gift for my favourite guest.
              I won't eat you now, but you'll be last, and best!

He laughs, then stamps about the stage in a kind of drunken, staggering dance, accompanied by a drumbeat.

2nd SAILOR   And he laughs and sways . . .

3rd SAILOR   And staggers, and reels . . .

1st SAILOR   Drunk on the wine . . .   270

My name's Noman *The Ancient Greek word for* noman *or* nobody *is* oudeis. *Odysseus, therefore, is making a play on his name, which is lost in translation.*

2nd SAILOR	Helpless, stumbling . . .
3rd SAILOR	Legless, tumbling . . .
Ist SAILOR	Until, like an oak tree torn up by its roots . . .
2nd SAILOR	Like a great boulder blasted by lightning . . .
3rd SAILOR	Like the mast of a ship cracked by a stormwind . . .
Ist SAILOR	The great, slobbering brute topples over . . .
2nd SAILOR	And crashes to the floor . . .
3rd SAILOR	Out for the count!

POLYPHEMOS crashes to the floor. The drumbeat comes to an abrupt stop.   280

NOMAN	Right! While he's out, this is what we do.

As they speak, now, they take up a wooden pole, which has been sharpened to a point.

Ist SAILOR	So he tells us his plan and we all jump to it.
2nd SAILOR	Grabbing a log from a stack of firewood . . .
3rd SAILOR	. . . half a tree trunk . . .
Ist SAILOR	. . . it takes all of us to lift it.
2nd SAILOR	Shaving one end to a sharp point . . .
3rd SAILOR	Then taking the weight . . .
NOMAN	Careful, now, lads! 290
Ist SAILOR	Raising it up . . .
NOMAN	Keep it steady!
2nd SAILOR	Carrying it forward . . .
NOMAN	Don't rush, now!
3rd SAILOR	Taking aim . . .
NOMAN	All together!

Ist SAILOR	One . . .
2nd SAILOR	Two . . .
3rd SAILOR	Three . . .
ALL	And ramming it deep in the monster's eye! 300

The SAILORS stab the pole into the eye, then all freeze, except for NOMAN, who speaks to the audience.

NOMAN   And I leaned my weight on it, turning it, twisting it, boring straight through that great eye socket, right down deep to the back of the skull. And the blood flowed, bubbling and hissing, and the Cyclops rose up, bellowing in pain.

All move again. The SAILORS drag the pole back and drop it down, and POLYPHEMOS roars out in agony, holding his hands to the blood wound in his face.   310

Ist SAILOR	He drags the spike from his eye!
2nd SAILOR	He claws at the gaping wound in his face!
3rd SAILOR	He stumbles in pain around the cave!
Ist SAILOR	Crashes into the walls!
2nd SAILOR	Sends goats and cheeses and milk-buckets flying!
3rd SAILOR	And cries aloud in his terrible agony!

POLYPHEMOS roars out again, then NOMAN speaks to the audience.

NOMAN   Then, from across the island, we heard others calling. Other Round-Eyes, far off, calling back to their brother.   320

We hear the voices of the other CYCLOPS calling out.

Ist CYCLOPS	What's the matter, Polyphemos?
2nd CYCLOPS	What's wrong, brother?
3rd CYCLOPS	Why do you cry out?

4th CYCLOPS	Has somebody hurt you?
5th CYCLOPS	Tell us. Who is it?
NOMAN	And that great, brainless, blind bulk of a brute called back . . .

POLYPHEMOS calls out.

POLYPHEMOS	Noman has blinded me! Noman has blinded me!	330
NOMAN	And when they heard that, his brothers called out . . .	
Ist CYCLOPS	No man's blinded you?	
2nd CYCLOPS	What's the trouble, then?	
3rd CYCLOPS	You've just had a bad dream.	
4th CYCLOPS	Stop all this shouting, Polyphemos.	
5th CYCLOPS	Go back to sleep, brother, and stop disturbing us from ours.	

The SAILORS and NOMAN all laugh.

Ist SAILOR	And when morning comes, he stumbles to the entrance.	340
2nd SAILOR	Rolls back the stone and lets out his goats.	
3rd SAILOR	And we go out with them, and he doesn't know we've gone.	
Ist SAILOR	Before he's any the wiser, we're back on the beach, pushing our ship into the shallows.	
2nd SAILOR	And we're onboard, and the mast's raised, and the sail's been set.	
3rd SAILOR	And we're heading off and away, out once more onto the wide open sea.	
NOMAN	As we pulled away, I looked back, and saw him, standing on the mountain-top. The sun was above him, and he was lit by its golden light, and he lifted his great, round,	350

blind eye to heaven, and cried out.

POLYPHEMOS calls out.

POLYPHEMOS   Father, Poseidon, Earth-Shaker! Hear my prayer!
Take revenge on the man who has wounded
        and maimed me.
Turn the waves against this Noman.
Ravage his ship with stormwinds.
Let the whole ocean become his enemy,   360
And death stalk him over the wide sea-ways.
Hear me, Poseidon. Grant this prayer.
For you are my father, and I am your son.

Ist SAILOR   His words crash like a curse upon us, their doom's drum
sounds in the ocean's deep.

2nd SAILOR   And we feel the sky's weight gathered above, and the
weight of the world grinding under our feet.

3rd SAILOR   And from that day on trouble rides in our wake, and we
wander the waves like rootless orphans.

Ist SAILOR   God-hunted, outcast . . .   370

2nd SAILOR   Refugee renegades . . .

3rd SAILOR   Marked for disaster and nameless death . . .

Ist SAILOR   No place to rest, no shelter or sanctuary . . .

2nd SAILOR   For Noman's our captain.

3rd SAILOR   And nowhere's our home.

 Father, Poseidon *Polyphemos was the child of the sea-god, Poseidon and
the sea nymph, Thoosa.*

ACTING In this scene, the sailors not only narrate what happens, they also enact it, using, for the most part, mime. With no scenery, and few, or no props, they must create what is happening visually at the same time as they are speaking.

In small groups, choose one of the sections below from the scene, and act it out, creating your own movements and mimes to go with the words:

a The opening section, up to where the sailors sleep on the beach

b The section where they climb up to the cave, beginning 'So we follow him' and ending 'And the path ends . . .'

DISCUSSION: NOMAN'S CHARACTER As a class, discuss why you think it is that Noman chooses to climb to the cave, to explore it, and to stay there, against all good advice. What does this tell you about his character?

Look at what Noman says in the scene, and discuss what more this tells you about his character.

ARTWORK: COSTUME DESIGN If you were designing this scene for the stage, how would you create Polyphemos, the Cyclops? Think about what effect you want the creature to have on the audience, and how you would best create this.

Would you have just one actor playing Polyphemos, or more than one?

Make a sketch of your costume design for Polyphemos, remembering that it must also be practical.

WRITING: CREATING AN EFFECT There are two dramatic effects needed in this scene. One is the effect of Polyphemos eating the two sailors, and the other is when Noman and his crew blind Polyphemos.

Look at the sections where these happen, then write notes on how you think this effect might best, and most simply, be created.

Keep in mind that, in the 'real' world of the play, this scene is being enacted by a group of travelling players, who would not have had with them any sophisticated materials.

LANGUAGE In the section where Polyphemos and Noman speak to each other, rhyming verse is used.

As a class, discuss why you think this is, and what effect this tries to create.

SCENE 3
Circe

EURYLOKHOS comes forward to join the others onstage. He speaks to the audience.

EURYLOKHOS	Bad weather blew us into unknown waters. Supplies were running short. But at last, the sea calmed, and we put into another island. We rested on the beach, then climbed to a headland above the sea. A great forest lay before us, and, out of the middle, a plume of smoke, rising.
NOMAN	We must find out who lives there.
EURYLOKHOS	*(Turns to NOMAN.)* But this time we'll be more cautious.
NOMAN	*(Turns to EURYLOKHOS.)* I agree. What do you suggest, Eurylokhos?
EURYLOKHOS	Divide the men into two bands. You take charge of one, I'll take the other. One band can stay with the ship, the other can go and explore.
NOMAN	How do we decide who stays and who goes?
EURYLOKHOS	Leave it to chance. Draw lots.
NOMAN	Good idea. Lets do it, then.
	NOMAN turns from EURYLOKHOS. EURYLOKHOS turns back to the audience. As he speaks, chorus of SAILORS enters.
EURYLOKHOS	The lot fell to my band, so we shouldered our weapons, and set off into the forest. We walked for a long time, then, at last, the trees opened out and we came to a wide glade. In the middle of the glade was a wooden house, lit by the sun. And on the grass around the house . . .
	A chorus of MAIDENS now approach and face the chorus of

The numbers 1, 10, and 20 appear in the right margin marking lines.

SAILORS. The MAIDENS are wearing animal masks . . . lion, wolf, bear, boar, fox, leopard and so on. Each MAIDEN also carries a pig-mask at her belt.

SAILORS   Lions, wolves, bears
They're hungry, ravenous
Their yellow eyes look murderous
And those terrible jaws   30
And the size of those claws
They'll tear us apart, limb from limb
This is no place for us
Quick, boys! Let's run!

They turn as one to go. MAIDENS speak.

MAIDENS   Stay. Don't go. There's nothing to fear.
We're not what we seem
Not savage or fierce or wild.
Our hearts are mild,
Our natures tame.   40
See how we slink, hear how we purr
Come closer, run your hands through our fur.
We won't bite.
Let the veils of terror fall from your sight,
Gaze on our true faces.

29

This is the place where your dreams
Come true,
Here, all pleasure and desire
Will be granted to you.

The MAIDENS take the animal masks from their faces.   50

SAILORS   Can you believe
What we're seeing?
Unless our eyes deceive us,
These aren't wild beasts, they're women!
What are such beauties doing here?
Is this an enchanted isle?
Who cares? Why fuss?
This place is for us,
Let's stay for a while.

EURYLOKHOS   And before I could stop them, they were off. But I stayed   60
behind, hiding in the trees, and I watched what happened.

*Gentle, haunting music plays. MAIDENS come forward, and
begin to encircle the SAILORS.*

MAIDENS   Come with us, take our hands
Be our guests in this welcome land,
Rest in the shade
Of our forest glade
Let all thought and memory fade.

The breeze is soft, the sun is warm,
Put behind you sea and storm   70
Rest in the shade
Of our forest glade
Let all thought and memory fade.

Let our kisses heal the scars
Of ancient, long-forgotten wars
Rest in the shade
Of our forest glade
Let all thought and memory fade.

Bathe in pools of golden light
The world's for pleasure and delight 80
Rest in the shade
Of our forest glade
Let all thought and memory fade.

The MAIDENS have now completely encircled the SAILORS, and the SAILORS can no longer be seen. Music stops.

EURYLOKHOS Then a woman came out of the house. The most beautiful woman I'd ever seen. She carried a gold-tipped staff in her hand, and she raised it above her head and called out.

CIRCE has turned to face the audience. She raises the staff she carries above her head, then brings it down with a thump. She 90 *chants.*

CIRCE Light One, O Bright One!
Great Mother of Mysteries!
Hear my supplication,
Circe, Dawn's daughter!

Let man come to beast,
Let him wear his true nature,
Earth's hated enemy,
Mankind the murderer!

Fuse finger and thumb, 100
Hoof hand and knuckle,
Hair sprout on skin,
Snout face and feature!

The MAIDENS join in with CIRCE's chant.

CIRCE Harmless we harness him,
MAIDENS Subdued in servitude

Great Mother of Mysteries *Circe is calling on the most ancient of powers, the nameless goddess of the earth, and mother of all.*

Dawn's daughter *Circe's father was Helios, the sun.*

CIRCE	Helpless we hold him
MAIDENS	Slave to our sisterhood
CIRCE	Beastlike we bind him
MAIDENS	Pet for our plaything 110
CIRCE/MAIDENS	Fresh meat for the table
	Fit creature for the sty!

CIRCE gives a final thump of the staff, and raises it triumphantly in the air. The MAIDENS part, to reveal the SAILORS, crouched, facing the audience, wearing pig-masks.

CIRCE   Take them in, sisters. Show our guests to their new homes.

The MAIDENS herd the pig-SAILORS off, who grunt and snort and squeal as they go. CIRCE turns and follows them. NOMAN now speaks to EURYLOKHOS.

NOMAN   Pigs?   120

EURYLOKHOS   Pigs. Every one of them.

NOMAN   What do you propose we should do, cousin?

EURYLOKHOS   Set sail and leave here, straight away.

NOMAN   And the men . . . the men you were given charge of?

EURYLOKHOS   There's nothing can be done for them.

NOMAN   I'm their captain. I have to try to do something.

EURYLOKHOS   Listen to me. You can't do anything against magic like that. That witch and her women are evil. If you go down there, you'll never come back.

NOMAN   Well, then, if by this time tomorrow I haven't returned,   130
you, as second-in-command, will take the rest of the men back onboard the ship and leave. Until then, rest here on the beach. It's the gods we're up against, and we have to be wary when dealing with them.

EURYLOKHOS goes. NOMAN turns from him, and HERMES enters and speaks to the audience.

HERMES   He never spoke a truer word. For always the gods are
                 watching. And at times, for some, they're waiting. Such was
                 the case with this man, Noman. No sooner had he set off
                 walking through the hushed woodland, than he found his   140
                 way barred by a shining figure with golden wand and
                 winged heels . . . me, Hermes, the messenger of the gods.

                 NOMAN turns and faces HERMES. HERMES speaks to him.

                 Where are you going, man? To your doom, you think?
                 If you were any man you might be
                 But you're not any man, you're Noman,
                 And that name's a favourite in the mouths of the gods.
                 The woman who lives here, whose home is this island
                 Is Circe the Sorceress, the Sun's daughter
                 Only she can tell you your one route home   150
                 But before she'll tell you, you have to show her
                 Just what kind of hero you are
                 Be the one man who can break her power.
                 Not an easy task for a mortal man
                 Unless he has some divine assistance.
                 And that's just what I bring you now.

                 HERMES holds out the leaves of a herb.

                 A herb this is, Moly it's called. You must eat it.
                 Chew it well, swallow it down. With its juices in your veins
                 Circe's magic will have no power over you,   160
                 You'll be protected from all her enchantments.
                 Then she'll do all you ask of her,
                 Treat you with honour, show you a good time.

Hermes – messenger of the gods *Hermes was not only the messenger of
the gods, but also the god who summoned men and women to their deaths
– as Odysseus finds out at the end of the play.*

Moly *Although it's uncertain, this was probably a species of wild garlic.
Garlic in many cultures is supposed to have magical powers, especially that
of warding off danger.*

And, with her help, you'll discover the way
Back to the known world, back to your own world.

*HERMES gives the herb to NOMAN. NOMAN eats it. HERMES
turns to the audience.*

He did all as I had bidden him, without question,
swallowed the herb, gave thanks, and went on his way. And
I, having done my job, went on mine, light as a breath,   **170**
back to Olympus, the dwelling-place of the gods, who,
unlike you mortals, know nothing of suffering, and never
die.

*HERMES goes. CIRCE enters to NOMAN, accompanied by her
MAIDENS. Their faces are hidden by hoods.*

CIRCE   What's this? Another visitor to our house? Another guest
for dinner? Approach, traveller. Don't be shy. Let Circe
show you her hospitality. Come, friend. Take my hand.
(Holds out her hand to him. He doesn't move.) No? What is it
you're afraid of? The touch of my flesh? Poor man, such   **180**
trials and terrors you must have undergone, to make you so
suspicious. Here, then. Take my staff.

*She holds out the end of her staff to NOMAN he hesitates, then
reaches out and takes it. As he does so, he drags CIRCE towards
him with it, holds it against her throat. She cries out.*

Sisters!

---

furies *Ancient female spirits of vengence, who pursued and tormented those
guilty of the murder of those of their own blood. They were pictured as
monstrous women with snakes for hair, and would hound and torment their
victim to death. In a story related to the* Odyssey, *when Agamemnon, leader
of the Greek expedition of Troy, returns home, he is murdered by his wife,
Klytemnestra. Some years later, their son, Orestes, kills his mother in revenge
for his father's death. He is pursued by the* **furies** *because he has spilled his
mother's blood, whereas she had been left alone, because Agamemnon was
only her husband, and not of her blood.*

The MAIDENS throw back their hoods to reveal themselves masked as FURIES. They screech with rage and advance.

NOMAN   Call off your Furies, witch! Call them off, or you die!

CIRCE   Back, sisters! Leave this man. He's not prey for you . . .   190
         not yet.

NOMAN   Nor ever will be. You think to turn me into a beast? Make
         me Chief Pig? Think again. There's no beast to be charmed
         from beneath my skin. I am what you see, a man all the
         way through, no more and no less. Your magic has no
         power over me.

CIRCE   If that's the case, you have nothing to fear from me.

NOMAN   No. Nothing at all.

CIRCE   Then let me go.

         He pauses a moment, then looses her. She steps away, turns to   200
         face him.

         Now, if the mighty conqueror will be so gracious, please
         hand me my staff.

         NOMAN gives her the staff. She takes it, and with a sudden
         movement, raises it as if to strike him with it, but then brings it
         down gently on his shoulder.

         Sisters, this is a true man. Show him your kinder faces.

         The MAIDENS remove their masks. CIRCE speaks to NOMAN.

         Take my hand, now, without mistrust or fear. Enter my
         house. There'll be good food and sweet wine, gentle music,   210
         fresh clothes. And other pleasures befitting a courageous
         warrior and leader of men.

NOMAN   First – release my men from their captivity.

CIRCE   As you so desire. *(To the MAIDENS.)* Bring out those
         mariners. And treat them with the honour that this man
         has earned. *(MAIDENS go. CIRCE turns to NOMAN.)* Your

coming here was foretold to me. I know your name and your desire. You wish to return home, but the way's lost to you.

NOMAN   I was told you could help me.   220

CIRCE   I can. Although your way is unknown to me, there's one to whom all destinations are known. He's the one you must seek.

NOMAN   Tell me who he is, and where I can find him.

CIRCE   Not yet. It's a hard journey, and a dark one. Only the bravest of hearts and the strongest of spirits can make it. You must rest here for a while, and find the strength you need. And not only a man's strength but a woman's as well. Woman and man, wedded together. Only by this will you achieve your heart's desire . . . an end to all trouble and a   230 swift road home.

She holds out her hand to him. He pauses, then takes it, and they go.

MAIDENS and SAILORS enter. Each MAIDEN carries a crown of flowers.

SAILORS   What's going on here?
What's all this about?
Our bodies feel as if they've been stretched
As if pulled apart
And then stuck clumsily back together.   240
Are we deranged,
Or did we really exchange
A face for a snout?

MAIDENS   There's really no need to be disturbed.
We said before, nothing here
Is as it seems.
Did no one ever tell you
All life is just a dream?
Nothing's certain or clear

Now the spell you   250
Were under is broken
And as token
Of our good intent, let each wear a crown
Of flowers woven lovingly by our own hands.

The MAIDENS raise the crowns of flowers.

Men and women weren't born
For strife and war.
The gods made us to be joined together,
Hand in glove
Like sister and brother.   260
Husband and wife,
Two halves of one whole,
In harmony and love.
One body, one soul.

*Each MAIDEN places a crown of flowers on the head of each
SAILOR. The two choruses speak together.*

MAIDENS/SAILORS With petal and blossom
Let strife be forgotten.
With flower and leaf
Let there be no more grief.   270
Life's brief as a breath
And destined for death
And the grave's yawning wide
For each groom and each bride.
So joy, love and pleasure
Are things we should treasure
And grasp while we can.
Every woman and man
They're gifts from above
Bestowed here to prove   280
Our hearts bound,
Our heads crowned,
Our souls drowned,
In love.

MAIDENS and SAILORS go, hand in hand. EURYLOKHOS enters, watching them go with some disdain, and then turns to the audience.

EURYLOKHOS A long time we stayed there. How long, I can't say. Time had no meaning on that island. But it was too long for my liking. Seeing the men, the way they behaved with those . . . women . . . more like love-sick goat-herds than warriors. And our captain was worse than all the rest put together!

NOMAN and CIRCE enter, hand in hand, gazing lovingly at each other. EURYLOKHOS turns to them.

When are we leaving, captain? Isn't it time we were on our way?

NOMAN speaks to EURYLOKHOS, without taking his eyes from CIRCE.

NOMAN Soon, Eurylokhos. Soon.

EURYLOKHOS turns back to the audience.

EURYLOKHOS He never even took his eyes from her face. It made me sick! He hadn't broken her power at all. She'd just exchanged one kind of magic for another. And it was always the same, the same answer whenever I asked him.

NOMAN Soon. We'll be going soon enough.

EURYLOKHOS I'd have left him there and taken the ship myself, but there was no one else to sail it. Not a single man. So, all I could do was just keep on at him, asking the same question, getting the same answer . . .

NOMAN Soon enough, Eurylokhos, soon enough . . .

EURYLOKHOS . . . day after day, not letting him rest, like a thorn in his foot, like a needle under his thumbnail, when are we going, when are we leaving here . . . ?

NOMAN suddenly turns to EURYLOKHOS and snaps.

290

300

31C

NOMAN	Now.	
EURYLOKHOS	What?	
NOMAN	The time's come.	
EURYLOKHOS	To leave . . . ?	
NOMAN	Yes.	320

EURYLOKHOS Not before time, if you don't mind my saying. I'll go and tell the others we'll be sailing with the tide . . .

NOMAN Not *we*, Eurylokhos. We're not sailing anywhere. I'm going alone.

EURYLOKHOS Alone?

NOMAN That's what I said.

EURYLOKHOS You're leaving us here?

NOMAN In the care of Circe, for the time being . . .

EURYLOKHOS Abandoning us . . . !

NOMAN No . . . !   330

EURYLOKHOS But you said . . .

NOMAN Listen to me, cousin. This next journey I'm making, I wouldn't ask anyone to come with me. It must be undertaken by one man, alone. But I'll come back to you, I promise, and when I do . . . then, with some luck and good fortune and a little cunning, we'll outwit the gods and make our voyage back home.

EURYLOKHOS I don't understand . . . I thought she was going to tell you the way back . . .

NOMAN There's only one man who knows how I can get back home, 340 and only Circe can send me to find him.

EURYLOKHOS Who is this man?

NOMAN Tiresias.

EURYLOKHOS	Tiresias? The Theban prophet . . . ?
NOMAN	Yes.
EURYLOKHOS	That's crazy. Tiresias is dead. He died long ago.
NOMAN	I know. But I must seek him out. Seek out his spirit. That's the journey I have to make. That's where Circe, with her magic arts, will send me. To the Land of Shadows, the place of the Dead.
EURYLOKHOS	No . . .
CIRCE	It must be. There is no other way.
EURYLOKHOS	You say . . .
CIRCE	Yes, I do say. And you would do well to heed my words, man, and remember who I am . . .
EURYLOKHOS	. . . a sorceress and a witch! *(To Noman.)* She's bewitched you! She'll send you to the Land of Shadows, and you'll never return.
NOMAN	If I don't you'll have to take your chances without me. Say no more, Eurylokhos. My mind's made up and my course is set.
	EURYLOKHOS turns to the audience.
EURYLOKHOS	So I left him, and went back to guard the ship. And as I sat there on deck alone, I thought of all those who had died, and whose spirits walked in the Land of Shadows, and of

350

360

Land of Shadows *Tartarus, the land of the dead lay beneath the earth, and was ruled over by Hades, another of Zeus's brothers, and his queen Persephone. Its entrance was a cave through which ran the river Styx. The souls of all who died, good or bad, were taken across the Styx by the ferryman, Charon, never to return to the world of light. Only a few mortals had ever dared to enter the land of the dead – Orpheus, Theseus and Herakles being the most well-known.*

him going there among them, and felt certain in my heart that he was lost and I'd never see him in this world again.

EURYLOKHOS goes.

CIRCE turns to NOMAN.

CIRCE   This last year you have walked in the country of the light.   370
You have been nourished by its power, which is the power of the sun. It had given you strength. You must now take that strength and that power into the country of the dark. You must look death in the face. Only then can you discover the one road that leads through death and back to your own world. Are you ready to take that journey?

NOMAN   I am.

CIRCE   Take it, then, with my love and blessing.

She kisses him on the forehead. Lights dim. Music plays. Drum and a flute, slow and solemn. The chorus of MAIDENS enter.   380
One carries a flame burning on a small dish, another bread, another a cup. NOMAN kneels. CIRCE stands above and behind him. The chorus stand in a semi-circle around him. The MAIDEN with the flame approaches him, and places the flame on the floor before him.

FLAME MAIDEN   Light the flame.

The MAIDEN with the bread approaches him, and hands it to him.

BREAD MAIDEN   Break the bread.

NOMAN breaks the bread, eats some of it. She takes the rest   390
back.

The MAIDEN with the cup approaches him. She gives him the cup.

CUP MAIDEN   Drink the blood.

NOMAN drinks from the cup and hands it back to her. All MAIDENS now speak.

MAIDENS   Wake the Dead.

They chant together.

Light the flame
Break the bread   400
Drink the blood
Wake the Dead

They repeat the chant, three times, their voices growing louder. After the third chant, they stop, and CIRCE cries out.

CIRCE   Kore! Persephone!
Daughter, Dark One
Kore! Persephone!
Mother of Earth
Kore! Persephone!
Lover of lost ones   410
Queen of the Night.

MAIDENS now join in this chant with CIRCE.

MAIDENS   Kore! Persephone!
CIRCE   Daughter, Dark One
MAIDENS   Kore! Persephone!
CIRCE   Mother of Earth
MAIDENS   Kore! Persephone!
CIRCE   Lover of lost ones
MAIDENS   Kore! Persephone!
CIRCE   Queen of the Night.   420

Kore! Persephone! *Persephone was the daughter of Demeter, goddess of growing things. She was abducted by Hades to be his queen, and ruled the Land of the Dead with him. Kore was her name before she was abducted, Persephone being the title she was given as queen of the dead.* Kore, *in Greek, means* daughter. Kore *is pronounced* 'KAW-REE'.

Chorus now divide into two. As they chant, they close a circle around NOMAN so that he cannot be seen.

MAIDEN	Kore! Persephone!
TWO MAIDENS	Light the flame!
CIRCE	Daughter, Dark One
TWO MAIDENS	Break the bread!
MAIDEN	Kore! Persephone!
TWO MAIDENS	Drink the blood!
CIRCE	Mother of Earth
TWO MAIDENS	Wake the Dead!
MAIDEN	Kore! Persephone!
TWO MAIDENS	Light the flame!
CIRCE	Lover of lost ones
TWO MAIDENS	Break the bread!
MAIDEN	Kore! Persephone!
TWO MAIDENS	Drink the blood!
CIRCE	Queen of the Night!
TWO MAIDENS	Wake the Dead!

430

This whole chant rises to a climax. Then, music and chanting stop, abruptly, and there is complete blackout.

LANGUAGE AND ACTING In this scene, the chorus of sailors and chorus of maidens speak in partly rhyming verse. This verse could be spoken in a variety of ways: whole chorus speaking lines together, separate lines being spoken individually, lines being spoken by groups of two and three and so on.

In groups, take one of these verse sections, and try speaking it in a number of ways, and decide which, for you, is the best way. Remember, there is no right or wrong way of doing this.

DISCUSSION: LANGUAGE When the god Hermes speaks to the audience, he speaks in prose. When he speaks to Noman, he speaks in blank (unrhyming) verse.

As a class, discuss why you think the playwright has chosen to use these two different forms of language for this character.

DISCUSSION AND WRITING: CHARACTER When you're acting a part in a play, it's important to understand a character's *motivation* – in other words, the reasons why he or she behaves and speaks as they do. In this scene, Circe's motives for behaving as she does are not immediately clear. In groups, discuss Circe's character and actions, looking at the following questions:

● What do you think are her reasons for being hostile to men?
● Do you think Noman really breaks her power? If not, why does she seem to give in to him?
● What do you think are her feelings towards Noman, and why does she decide to help him?
● Why does she keep him with her on her island for so long, before sending him on to the land of the dead?

After your discussions, make notes on Circe's character, that would be useful for an actor who would be playing her.

ARTWORK Make a sketch of what you think one of the masks in the scene would look like – either one of the animal masks, or one of the Fury masks.

Make notes on what materials it would be made of, and how it would be worn, remembering that these masks have to be taken on and off quickly and easily.

WRITING Imagine you're Eurylokhos, waiting by the ship, after Noman has gone to the Land of the Dead.
● Do you think Noman will ever return?
● Do you think you'll ever get back home?

Write a short monologue, in prose or poetry, showing your thoughts and feelings about the whole episode.

DISCUSSION: CREATING A RITUAL The final section of this scene is a magic ritual performed in order to send Noman to the Land of the Dead. The words are only one part of the ritual. For it to have its most powerful effect on the audience, music and movement should also be part of the ritual.

In small groups, discuss how you would create this magic ritual, what kind of music and movement you'd use, any special costume or props or effects you might want, whether you'd have the words chanted or sung, or both.

After the discussion, either make notes, or sketches, or both, showing how you would stage this ritual.

SCENE 4
The Land of Shadows

A single, dim light rises on two figures, seated, cross-legged on the floor, facing each other . . . TIRESIAS and TIRESIA, male and female. Both are dressed exactly alike, and both have a cloth tied over their eyes. Each has a wooden staff. They are playing a game with small bones. First, TIRESIA shakes the bones, scatters them on the floor.

TIRESIA	You win.	1

TIRESIAS scoops up the bones, shakes them, scatters them on the floor.

TIRESIAS　　　You win.

TIRESIA once more takes up the bones, shakes them, scatters them.

TIRESIA/TIRESIAS　　We both win.

They laugh.

TIRESIA　　　We never lose.

TIRESIAS　　It's impossible.　　　　　　　　　　　10

TIRESIA　　　Play again?

TIRESIAS　　Why not?

TIRESIA　　　We have plenty of time.

TIRESIAS　　All the time.

Tiresias . . . Tiresia *The story of why Tiresias is both male and female is told later in the scene. In the* Odyssey *Odysseus meets Tiresias only in his male form. The idea of having both male and female forms exist at the same time is unique to this dramatisation.*

TIRESIA	Nothing but . . .
TIRESIAS/TIRESIA	. . . time.

TIRESIAS takes up the bones, shakes them, is about to throw them, when TIRESIA reaches out and takes his hand.

TIRESIA	Someone's coming.

They cock their heads, listen, sniff the air.   20

TIRESIAS	Flesh.
TIRESIA	Blood.
TIRESIAS	Guts.
TIRESIA	Bone.
TIRESIAS	Mortal man.
TIRESIA	Doomed to die.

NOMAN enters.

TIRESIAS	Someone's here.
TIRESIA/TIRESIAS	Noman's here.

NOMAN approaches them. TIRESIAS offers the bones to him.   30

TIRESIAS	Play.
TIRESIA	Throw.

NOMAN takes the bones. He throws them.

TIRESIAS	You lose.
TIRESIA	We win.
TIRESIAS	We always win.
TIRESIA	We never lose.
TIRESIAS	It's impossible.
TIRESIA	Play again?

NOMAN	No.	40
TIRESIAS	Never mind.	
TIRESIA	Another time.	
TIRESIAS	There's always another time.	
TIRESIA	Always plenty of . . .	
TIRESIA/TIRESIAS	. . . time.	
NOMAN	Tell me . . .	
TIRESIA	You tell us, man . . .	
TIRESIAS	. . . mortal man . . .	
TIRESIA	Tell us, mortal man, what are you doing here?	
TIRESIAS	In Death's Kingdom?	50
TIRESIA	In Death's Dream Kingdom.	
TIRESIAS	What is it you're seeking here?	
NOMAN	I'm looking for . . . Tiresias.	
TIRESIA	The Theban prophet.	
TIRESIAS	The blind seer.	
TIRESIA	Looking for him.	
TIRESIAS	Looking for her.	
TIRESIA	He's here.	
TIRESIA	She's here.	
NOMAN	Where?	60
TIRESIAS	Here.	
TIRESIA	Here.	
TIRESIAS/TIRESIA	Here.	
NOMAN	Two of you?	

TIRESIAS	Two.
TIRESIA	And one.
TIRESIAS	Two.
TIRESIA	Is one.
TIRESIAS	Male.
TIRESIA	And female.
TIRESIAS	Man.
TIRESIA	And woman.
TIRESIAS	Don't you know the story?
TIRESIA	Shall we tell him the story?
TIRESIAS	Will he listen?
TIRESIA	He has no choice.
TIRESIAS/TIRESIA	We'll tell him the story.

They stand and tell the story, enacting it as they do.

TIRESIAS	A long time ago . . .
TIRESIA	On a warm, spring morning . . .
TIRESIAS	I'm walking in the mountains . . .
TIRESIA	When I see two snakes . . .
TIRESIAS	Male and female . . .
TIRESIA	Coupling together . . .
TIRESIAS	Writhing and knotting their passion in the dust.
TIRESIA	Disgusting!
TIRESIAS	Revolting!
TIRESIA	I strike out with my staff!

TIRESIAS strikes down with his staff.

70

80

TIRESIAS	Kill one of the snakes . . .	90
TIRESIA	The female snake.	
TIRESIAS	And instantly I'm transformed!	
TIRESIA	And become a woman! For seven years I live as a woman. No longer Tiresias, but Tiresia. Gracious and beautiful. All the young men desire me. And I desire them. I forget that ever I was a man.	
TIRESIAS	And then, one day, on a warm spring morning , I'm walking in the mountains, when I see two snakes . . .	
TIRESIA	Male and female . . .	
TIRESIAS	Coupling together . . .	100
TIRESIA	Writhing and knotting their passion in the dust.	
TIRESIAS	Disgusting!	
TIRESIA	Revolting!	
TIRESIAS	I strike out with my staff!	

TIRESIAS strikes down with her staff.

TIRESIA	Kill one of the snakes!	
TIRESIAS	The male snake.	
TIRESIA	And instantly I'm transformed!	
TIRESIAS	And become a man again. But the woman's not forgotten, she's still here inside me.	110
TIRESIA	She me . . .	
TIRESIAS	. . . and I her.	
TIRESIA	Two of us in one skin.	
TIRESIAS	And that night, I have a dream.	
TIRESIA	Two snakes appear, but I know they're two gods . . .	

TIRESIAS	Zeus, the All-Father . . .
TIRESIA	Hera, the All-Mother . . .
TIRESIAS	And these two gods, they ask me a question.
TIRESIA	In lovemaking . . .
TIRESIAS	Says Hera . . .

120

TIRESIA	Who has the greater pleasure? Is it the man or the woman? I say it's the man.
TIRESIAS	Whereas I . . .
TIRESIA	Says Zeus . . .
TIRESIAS	. . . say it's the woman. Settle this argument for us, Tiresias. You, of all mortals, should know the answer to this.
TIRESIA	So I consider, and then I give my answer.
TIRESIAS	In my experience, it's the woman. Definitely the woman who finds the most pleasure.
TIRESIA	Liar!

130

TIRESIAS	Screams Hera . . .
TIRESIA	Your tongue spits falsehood! You see no truth! From this time on, Tiresias, be blind!
TIRESIAS	And she takes out my eyes and plunges me into darkness.

Both TIRESIA and TIRESIAS clasp their hands over their faces and scream.

TIRESIA	But Zeus is kinder. Zeus approaches me, in human form now, and touches with his fingers the holes where my eyes were.
TIRESIAS	Where you cannot see the present, see the future. Read with inner eyes the maps of what is to come.

140

Both slowly take their hands from their faces.

TIRESIA	So I became what I am.
TIRESIAS	What I was, in the upper world.
TIRESIA	The world of light.
TIRESIAS	The world of life.
TIRESIAS	Soft breeze and birdsong . . .
TIRESIA	Warm sunlight on skin . . .
TIRESIAS	Your world, man. The world you left to come here.
TIRESIA	To seek me out and ask the question . . .

150

TIRESIAS	How shall I get back home?

They sit again, as before.

NOMAN	And will you tell me the answer? How shall I get back home? What further dangers await me? How shall I overcome them? Only you know. Only you can say.

TIRESIAS throws the bones.

TIRESIAS	You must pass by the island of the Sirens.

Lights rise on the TWO SIRENS.

LEUKOSIA	Earth's daughters.
AGLAOPE	Persephone's playmates.

160

LEUKOSIA	When she was stolen by Hades we went looking for her.
AGLAOPE	All over the earth, but we couldn't find her.
LEUKOSIA	We prayed to our mother, she gave us wings.
AGLAOPE	We became bird-women, searching the wide ocean.

 the two sirens *The actual number of sirens varies from myth to myth.*

LEUKOSIA	We called for her, we couldn't find her.
AGLAOPE	She was gone from the world, queen of the shadow-lands.
LEUKOSIA	Our call became a song, haunting the sea-waves.
AGLAOPE	We came to an island and rested there.
LEUKOSIA	We rest there still, calling, singing.
AGLAOPE	A song so beautiful you can't resist it.
LEUKOSIA	You leap from your ship, you swim towards us.
AGLAOPE	And gently, lovingly, we take you apart.
LEUKOSIA	Feast on your flesh, leave your bones on the rocks.

170

Lights off the TWO SIRENS.

TIRESIA	Death's their song. Plug your ears to it.
TIRESIAS	Or, if you wish to hear it and live, bind yourself hard to the ship's mast.

TIRESIA scoops up and throws the bones.

TIRESIA	You'll come to the twin dangers of the serpent and the whirlpool.

180

Lights rise on KHARYBDIS and SKYLLA.

KHARYBDIS	Kharybdis, Poseidon's daughter.
SKYLLA	Skylla, daughter of the night.
KHARYBDIS	I was born with an appetite that couldn't be satisfied.
SKYLLA	Poseidon desired me, and took me for his lover,
KHARYBDIS	God flung me out of heaven, into the ocean.
SKYLLA	Circe was jealous, she turned me into a monster.
KHARYBDIS	Now I lie on the ocean-bed, my hunger still ravenous.
SKYLLA	Chained me to a rock, gave me a taste for human flesh.

KHARYBDIS	I suck in the ocean, and any ship that sails on it.	190
SKYLLA	I pounce from my cave, my dragon's mouth howling.	
KHARYBDIS	And men's bones lie silent in the sea's deep.	
SKYLLA	And men's bones lie silent on the black rock.	

Lights off SKYLLA and KHARYBDIS.

TIRESIAS	The channel between these two is narrow.	
TIRESIA	Steer a steady course through it if you wish to reach home.	

TIRESIAS scoops up and throws the bones.

TIRESIAS	Most dangerous of all, are the Cattle of the Sun.	

Lights rise on HELIOS, the sun-god.

HELIOS	Helios, the Sun Titan. Older than gods, born from the great mother at the world's beginning. In my chariot of light I drive the sun across the sky, bring warmth and life to the world of men. Like the sun my cattle are golden, they graze the green pastures of the island Sicily, they are sacred to me, and their meat is forbidden.	200

Lights off HELIOS.

TIRESIA	Leave those cattle unharmed, and you'll end your journey safely.	
TIRESIAS	Harm them, and the ocean will tumble about you.	
NOMAN	And then? *(They don't reply.)* After I get back home? *(They say nothing.)* Is all well there? Or does further trouble await	210

Helios, the Sun Titan *The Titans were a race of giants that ruled creation before the gods, and were overthrown by Zeus and his family in the great war in heaven. Many of them were imprisoned in Tartarus. Helios, as the Titan who drove the sun across the sky from dawn to dusk in his fiery chariot, did not fight against the gods, and retained his standing and power.*

me? *(They still don't answer.)* What will happen after I get back home?

TIRESIA	We've told you all you need to know.
TIRESIAS	All you came to know.
TIRESIA	You know enough.
TIRESIAS	Don't seek to know more.
NOMAN	But I do. I do seek to know more.
TIRESIA	This isn't what you're here for.
TIRESIAS	It's not part of the bargain.
NOMAN	I made no bargain.
TIRESIA	You did, the moment you entered this place.
TIRESIAS	All make a bargain who enter this place.
TIRESIA	Give . . .
TIRESIAS	. . . and take . . .
TIRESIA	. . . win . . .
TIRESIAS	. . . and lose . . .
NOMAN	I want to know. Tell me! I want to know my destiny!
TIRESIA	He wants to know.
TIRESIAS	His destiny.
TIRESIA	He demands to know.
TIRESIAS	His destiny.

220

230

TIRESIA scoops up the bones, offers them to NOMAN.

TIRESIA	Here. Seek it yourself.

NOMAN takes the bones. He throws them.

Pause.

NOMAN	Well? What do you see?
TIRESIAS	Death.
TIRESIA	Death.
TIRESIAS	Death will come for you.
TIRESIA	As it comes for all who live under the sun.
TIRESIAS	On a fine day when the weather's warm . . .
TIRESIA	And the waves wash gently over the rocks . . .
TIRESIAS	A young man comes walking out of the sea.
	A GHOST-FIGURE enters, carrying a spear. He approaches NOMAN.
TIRESIA	You look up from your sleep, see him standing above you.
TIRESIAS	The sun's behind him, and his face is in shadow.
TIRESIA	You ask who he is, his name, his country.
TIRESIAS	And he answers this, a single word.
GHOST-FIGURE	Noman.
TIRESIA	His name.
GHOST-FIGURE	Noman.
TIRESIAS	Your name.

240

55

GHOST-FIGURE	Noman.

The GHOST-FIGURE raises his spear. TIRESIA and TIRESIAS speak together.

TIRESIA/TIRESIAS	As we are now, so you shall be
	When Death comes walking from the sea 270
	And reaches out and takes your hand
	And leads you here to the Shadowlands.

The GHOST-FIGURE is poised to cast his spear at NOMAN. In a fear and terror that has been growing steadily, he falls to his knees, throws up his arms for protection, and cries out.

NOMAN	No!

His cry plunges all into darkness.

Pause.

A light rises, to reveal TIRESIA and TIRESIAS seated as before. Nearby, NOMAN kneels, his head covered by his arms. The   280 GHOST-FIGURE is gone.

TIRESIA	It's all right, now. It's over.
TIRESIAS	All done with. You can go.

NOMAN lifts his head, looks around, stands.

TIRESIA	You've learned what you came here to learn. And a little bit more. You're lucky.
TIRESIAS	Normally, when men overstep the mark, they're punished for their audacity.
TIRESIA	Blasted by thunderclap.
TIRESIAS	Seared by a lightning bolt. 290
TIRESIA	But not you. You must be highly favoured.

NOMAN doesn't move.

TIRESIAS	Well? What are you waiting for? Don't push your luck.

TIRESIA	The gods will be tempted only so far.	
TIRESIAS	Stay any longer, and Persephone might take a fancy to you.	
TIRESIA	Decide to keep you here forever.	
TIRESIAS	So I should go now, while you still can.	
NOMAN	Is there . . . any payment to be made?	
TIRESIA	Payment? Of course there's a payment.	
TIRESIAS	There's always a payment.	300
TIRESIA	Everything costs.	
TIRESIAS	Nothing's for free.	
TIRESIA	But not now. You don't have to pay it now.	
TIRESIAS	Later. You'll pay when the time comes.	
TIRESIA	Everyone pays when the time comes.	
TIRESIAS	Go on, now. Back to your own world. For the time being.	
TIRESIA	We'll see you again. You can be sure of that.	

NOMAN steps towards them as if to speak to them, changes his mind, turns, and goes.

TIRESIAS	Shall we play?	310
TIRESIA	Yes. Let's play.	
TIRESIAS	Who first?	
TIRESIA	You.	

TIRESIAS casts the bones.

TIRESIAS	You win.	
TIRESIA	We both win.	
TIRESIAS	We never lose.	
TIRESIA	It's impossible.	

TIRESIAS	Play again?	
TIRESIA	Why not?	320
TIRESIAS	We have plenty of time.	
TIRESIA	All the time.	
TIRESIAS	Nothing but . . .	
TOGETHER	. . . time.	

TIRESIAS scoops up the bones and throws them.

Lights fade to blackout.

ACTING As in some other scenes, a *narrative theatre* device is used in this scene, when Tiresias and Tiresia tell Noman their story.

In this section, the actors playing these two characters have to do three things:

i tell the story
ii play themselves in the story
iii play Zeus and Hera in the story.

This requires the actors to perform in three slightly different ways, in order to keep the section clear.

a In twos, try acting out this section, and see what different ways you can find of staging it, and making it work.

b Work towards a prepared performance, and share your work with other pairs.

c After you've done this, discuss each pairs' work.

ARTWORK: WRITING If you were staging this scene for the theatre, how would you try to create the atmosphere of the Land of the Dead? Either make a sketch, with notes, or write a description of your staging ideas.

FINDING OUT: CHARACTER When Tiresias was alive, in the city of Thebes, he was a highly regarded and honoured figure, and regarded as one of the greatest of prophets. He features in many myths, the two most well-known being the story of *Oedipus,* and the story of *Pentheus and Dionysos.*

Find out what you can about these two myths, and the role Tiresias plays in them, and see how this might add to your understanding of the character of Tiresias/Tiresia as portrayed in this scene.

SCENE 5
Sea Perils

Lights rise to NOMAN standing central, gazing outwards, as if in a trance-like state.
ZEUS enters, apart from NOMAN.

ZEUS   Time to begin again.

HERA enters.

HERA   Time to resume the hazardous journey.

POSEIDON enters.

POSEIDON   Time to plunge this man into further perils.

ATHENA enters.

ATHENA   Time to test to the limit his resources and his skill.

APOLLO enters.

APOLLO   Time to bring all things to their appointed end.

The GODS form a semi-circle around NOMAN, possibly on a   10
raised area, but with easy access to the main stage. The effect is
of the GODS directing, and being in complete control of,
NOMAN's destiny.

ZEUS   Let him leave Circe's enchanted and enchanting island . . .

HERA   An island to be found on no map, because, like all things
divine and eternal, it exists only in the divine, eternal . . .

POSEIDON   Let him set sail once more across the open sea, chart a
course through the Zodiac of our imagined world . . .

 Zodiac *In the ancient world, the Zodiac was that region of the sky where
heaven was located and guarded by mythical or semi-mythical creatures
such as the scorpion. Odysseus is now in this magical otherworld of the gods
– the Zodiac.*

ATHENA	While we watch, from heaven, temporarily charmed by the audacity of this man, thrilled by his courage, beguiled by his daring, amused and intrigued by the outcome of his fate . . .

20

APOLLO	Which we, being gods, divine and eternal, have already plotted well in advance.

They laugh at this joke.

ZEUS	First, then . . . the Sirens.

ZEUS claps his hands. AGLAOPE and LEUKOSIA, the SIRENS, enter, wearing their bird-masks, and cloaked with feathers. They speak, softly, gently, as music plays, attempting to entrance NOMAN.

30

AGLAOPE	Hear us, Noman, hear our song.
LEUKOSIA	The song of the Sirens, that only you can hear.
AGLAOPE	Bird-women, harp-throated.
LEUKOSIA	Hell's darling sisters.
AGLAOPE	Hear our song of longing, of the soul's sweet ache.
LEUKOSIA	Let it bind you.
AGLAOPE	Let it wrap you.
LEUKOSIA	Let it hold you fast.
AGLAOPE	Let it hug you in its arms like a mother hugs her baby.
LEUKOSIA	Her little man, her very own.

40

AGLAOPE	Her darling joy, her only love.
LEUKOSIA	Let it kiss you and caress you, let it soothe you to sleep.
AGLAOPE	Dream of an island where the bloom never fades.
LEUKOSIA	The island of the Sirens, beyond the world's edge.
AGLAOPE	The island of apples, where nothing's forbidden.

LEUKOSIA	Become lord of that land, its king and its priest.
AGLAOPE	Become one with that land.
LEUKOSIA	Let flesh melt to earth.
AGLAOPE	Let breath become breeze.
LEUKOSIA	Become bone on the shore.
AGLAOPE	Hear us, Noman, hear our song.
LEUKOSIA	The song of the Sirens, the song of the skull.

50

The SIRENS are now closing in on NOMAN, who is almost completely under their spell, then, as if dragging himself out of his trance, he gives a cry.

NOMAN   No!

The SIRENS, give a horrible, raucous screech of rage and dismay, then go. NOMAN once more turns and gazes outwards. The gods, except for ZEUS, laugh and applaud.

HERA   Well done! There's more to this man than mere flesh and bone.

60

POSEIDON   Shall we test him further? Probe a little deeper? Find what more he's made of?

ATHENA   Of course. That's what we're here for. That's what he's here for. He's our plaything, our pastime.

APOLLO   Our little butterfly. What shall we skewer him with this time?

ZEUS   Whatever you wish.

He turns to HERA.

My dear? Perhaps you have some thoughts.

70

HERA   One or two, my love. Let's stir up Kharybdis, the whirlpool.

KHARYBDIS enters, with swirling ribbons. She dances wildly around NOMAN, creating the effect of wild, swirling water. Once more, NOMAN snaps out of his trance. He calls out, as if to his crew.

NOMAN   Hold fast to your oars, men. Pull hard to starboard! Keep that rudder steady! Away from the whirlpool! Do you want to be meat for the fishes! Put your backs into it! To starboard! Hard over! Pull! Pull!

HERA   And, just for good measure, wake Skylla, the sea-monster.   80

SKYLLA appears, a terrible monster with several dog-heads that writhe and twist. NOMAN calls out again.

NOMAN   Pull over! Back to larboard! Keep out of the beast's reach! We can make it, boys! Just keep your heads and pull like fury! There's death on one side and destruction on the other, but it's sweet life and home on the path between the two. Keep going, boys! Don't look back! We've almost done it, almost left those devils behind! Let her fly, straight and clean, out of danger and rough water and away to a calm sea!   90

NOMAN'S voice rises to a cry of triumph. HERA cries out at the same time.

HERA	Enough!
	SKYLLA and KHARYBDIS withdraw. NOMAN returns to his trance-like state.
ZEUS	You were right, dear sister-wife. There is more to this man. A master mariner he is indeed.
POSEIDON	Master mariner he may be, but he won't master my ocean, nor all the creatures in it!
ZEUS	Thunder as much as you like, brother, but I don't think you'll so easily shake this man from the earth.
ATHENA	He's subtle and skilful, has a mind given to strategy. We too must be subtle if he's truly to suffer.
APOLLO	And suffer he must. He was born to it. Born to suffer, like all men.
HERA	For only through suffering can they come to wisdom.
ZEUS	Only through suffering can they come to truth.
POSEIDON	For man must suffer, suffer into truth.
ATHENA	And what is the truth man must suffer to learn?
APOLLO	That man was born to suffer.
	They applaud and laugh at the joke.
ZEUS	What further suffering for him, then. *(To ATHENA.)* Daughter? Do you have a suggestion?
ATHENA	Oh, yes! Let his ship put in to safe harbour. Some peaceful island resting in the warm sea.

100

110

man must suffer, suffer into truth *This is a line from Aeschylus's play* Agamemnon, *written in 458BC, about the murder of Agamemnon at the hands of his wife Klytemnestra.*

She rises, approaches NOMAN, and brushes her hand gently across his eyes. He closes his eyes.

Let him sleep there, let him have sweet dreams.

She kisses NOMAN on the forehead. NOMAN lets his head sink forward.   120

APOLLO   He thinks he's safe, now. All dangers past.

ZEUS   Almost home, he can smell it, the sweet smell of home.

HERA   That's when you get a man, when he's at his weakest.

POSEIDON   Give him hope, and then snatch it away.

APOLLO   That's the way to really twist in the knife.

ATHENA   And here, on this island, this haven of hope, we'll twist that knife so deep that it hurts.

She claps her hands.

Because here, grazing on this island, are the Cattle of the Sun.   130

Four PLAYERS enter, carrying above their heads, great curved pairs of golden horns.

ZEUS   The cattle he's been told he must not touch.

HERA   Don't hurt or harm them, and you'll get back home.

POSEIDON   And he's told his men not to hurt or harm them. And he sleeps, certain they'll obey his word.

ATHENA   He's their captain, their commander. They always obey him.

APOLLO   Except this time. This one time they won't. And it'll be the last time they don't.

Four SAILORS enter, in a trance-like state. Each SAILOR carries   140
a knife. The approach the CATTLE, as the GODS speak.

ZEUS   They're hungry. They're famished.

HERA	They haven't eaten meat for weeks.
POSEIDON	And here are all these cattle roaming about.
ATHENA	These beautiful cattle. These fat cattle.
APOLLO	And it won't hurt, will it, to kill just one?

The four sailors raise their knives

| ZEUS | Cut its throat, spill its blood. |

The first SAILOR cuts the throat of one of the CATTLE. It falls.

| HERA | Skin it, butcher it. | 150 |

The second SAILOR cuts the throat of another of the CATTLE. It falls.

| POSEIDON | Rip out its guts, chop up its flesh. |

The third SAILOR cuts the throat of another of the CATTLE. It falls.

| ATHENA | Build a fire, cook it, eat it. |

The fourth SAILOR cuts the throat of the last of the cattle. It falls.

| APOLLO | And he wakes to the smell of roasting meat. Burning flesh. His own. In hell. | 160 |

NOMAN jerks up his head, opens his eyes.

The GODS encircle him, crying out, accusing.

ZEUS	You've disobeyed the command of the gods.
HERA	Scorned the word and law of heaven.
POSEIDON	Broken the pact between man and the immortals.
ATHENA	Spurned the divine, turned your back on the sacred.
APOLLO	Stepped out far beyond acceptable limits.
ZEUS	Likewise, man, we turn our backs on you.

HERA	You can no longer count on our friendship or protection.
APOLLO	Disobedience must be punished, an example must be made. 170
ATHENA	From this time forth be outcast, outlaw.
POSEIDON	Unloved, hunted down, drowned in the storm of our wrath!

Sudden, loud, crashing drumbeat. We hear the VOICES of the storm calling out.

STORM VOICES
Wind howl!
Thunder crack!
Wave crash!
Storm wrack!

Ocean boom!
Fire spit!   180
Sea rise!
Earth split!

The chant is repeated over and over, growing louder, more furious. The storm VOICES close in on NOMAN as they chant, threatening to engulf him. But suddenly, he raises his head and cries out.

NOMAN
No!

At his cry, chant and drumbeat cease, abruptly. There is silence, as the storm VOICES fall back.

Then, NOMAN turns and accuses the GODS.   190

No. I will not die. I will not submit to your will. I refute your jurisdiction over my life. Do you hear me, you gods? Zeus, all-father. Hera, queen-sister. Poseidon, earth-shaker. Athena, wise warrior. Apollo, bright singer. Hear my voice,

Zeus – all father *See the section on The Greek Gods*

the voice of Noman. I am no god's plaything or puppet. I am myself, alone. From this time on, I'll make my own destiny. I have no more need of you. I defy you, and reject you. Let heaven be silent and empty. I am Noman, and all men, and the world's mine alone to walk in forever!

The GODS stare at him in silence; one by one, they turn, and go.   **200**

NOMAN is left alone. He speaks to the audience.

Let the skies clear. Let the waters calm. Let the sailor at last come home from the sea.

He stands on stage, central.

 DISCUSSION: ARTWORK Imagine you're staging this scene for the theatre. In small groups, discuss how you would costume the gods to make them sufficiently different from the other characters . Discuss how you would indicate to an audience which god was which. After your discussion, make sketches of your ideas, and add notes if necessary.

DISCUSSION As a class, discuss what you think is the attitude of the gods to Noman and his plight.
- Why do you think they are putting him through so much torment?
- Why do they appear to be so hostile to him?
- Is there hostility directed just towards Noman, or to humankind in general?
- If that's the case, why do you think the Greeks saw the world in this way?

FREEZE-FRAME Noman encounters four perils in this scene: the Sirens, Skylla and Kharybdis, the Cattle of the Sun, and a storm and shipwreck.
In small groups, create a freeze-frame for each of these perils, depicting what you think is the most dramatic moment of each.
You can then go on to make a sketch of each freeze-frame, as if you were creating a storyboard for a film. For each frame, make notes on what you want the audience to be hearing, and what the camera should be doing, e.g. moving in from longshot to close-up, showing a medium shot of the whole scene.

DISCUSSION At the end of the scene, Noman defies the gods, and declares that from now on he does not need them, and will be master of his own fate. The gods leave, and appear to be defeated.
As a class, discuss whether you think Noman really has defeated the gods, or if you think he is still really under their control.

SCENE 6
How Death Came to Ithaka

NOMAN now speaks to the audience. As he does so, lights come up on the audience on Ithaka.

NOMAN
I survived the shipwreck. I alone was saved. The storm was 　1
past, the sky was clear, I clung to the broken tiller, floated
for days on the open sea. Sharks swam by me, gentle as
sheep. Sea-hawks passed overhead, their beaks sheathed. At
last, a ship came by, saw me, pulled me from the water. It
was a trading ship, so I travelled with them, from island to
island, port to port. I worked my passage. Hard work, it was,
but hard work in the real world. No more monsters or
witches, no more dragons or gods. Just the creak of timber,
the slap of sail, the hum of rope, the company of men. And 　10
at length, the ship's passage brought it to familiar waters,
the known seas of my own homeland. We put into a
harbour, and I said farewell, and stepped ashore, at last, in
my own country.

Other PLAYERS now come forward, addressing the audience of SUITORS.

I survived the shipwreck *In Homer's* Odyssey, *after the shipwreck, Odysseus is washed up on the island of Ogygia, where he's cared for by the nymph Calypso. She keeps him there for seven years until Hermes, acting on Zeus's orders, tells her to release him. Odysseus builds a boat, which is again wrecked in a storm, and he's washed up this time on the island of Scheria – probably modern Corfu. But now he's back in the real world, and the king of the island sends him, with much treasure, in one of his own ships back to Ithaka. For the purposes of this play, none of this material has been used – although it's likely that it's on Scheria that he acquires his band of travelling players.*

1st PLAYER	So ends the story of Noman the Sailor.
2nd PLAYER	And so ends the play we have made of it.
3rd PLAYER	And if our play has pleased you . . .
4th PLAYER	If it has enthralled and thrilled you . . .
5th PLAYER	Amused, bemused and, at times, amazed you . . .
6th PLAYER	If our poor play has enriched the time . . .
7th PLAYER	Then we, poor players that we are . . .
8th PLAYER	Do beseech and implore you to grant us some little reward . . .
9th PLAYER	Some scraps of meat begged from your table . . .
10th PLAYER	Some dregs drained from your cup . . .
11th PLAYER	And perhaps a little money to see us safely on our way.
12th PLAYER	But more than all of these, your own warm hands to warm our humble hearts.

20

30

There is a moment's perplexed silence. Then, ANTINOÖS speaks.

ANTINOÖS	They mean they want us to applaud.

All applaud, the SUITORS briefly, lightly, the others with more enthusiasm. The PLAYERS all bow. But, they do not move from where they stand.

EURYMAKHOS	Is that it, then? Is it over?
AMPHIMEDON	It seems to be.
EURYDAMAS	Thank goodness for that. I thought it would never end.
LEOKRITOS	I quite enjoyed some of it.
LEODES	The bits you saw when you weren't asleep.
ANTINOÖS	And now that this . . . entertainment is concluded, perhaps we can get on with the real business of the day. The choosing of a husband.

40

He stands and begins to address PENELOPE.

Lady Penelope . . .

TELEMAKHOS	Wait. Aren't you forgetting something?
ANTINOÖS	Am I?
TELEMAKHOS	The players . . .
EURYMAKHOS	Them? They're easily forgotten.
AMPHIMEDON	And best forgotten.
TELEMAKHOS	But they are still here . . .
ANTINOÖS	It hadn't escaped my attention.

Turns to MELANTHIOS.

Melanthios. Escort these . . . players from the hall. And attend to them as they deserve.

MELANTHIOS	They'll be treated as they deserve all right.

MELANTHIOS stands.

TELEMAKHOS	What about their payment?
ANTINOÖS	Payment?
TELEMAKHOS	They deserve some reward . . .
ANTINOÖS	And they've had it – our attention – which was difficult to hold – and our appreciation – which was more than they deserve. For the rest, if they wish to wait outside until the celebrations here are finished, they're free to share the scraps with the dogs.
LEOKRITOS	Send them on their way. We've wasted too much time on them already. Lady Penelope lacks a husband, and Ithaka lacks a king.
LEODES	Melanthios. You've had your orders. Get rid of these scum.

MELANTHIOS turns to the PLAYERS.

50

60

70

MELANTHIOS	You heard the lords. Out, all of you.

The PLAYERS do not move.

Out!

They do not move.

Did you hear what I said? Out with you . . . !

He goes to push one of the PLAYERS. NOMAN grabs him, lifts him, throws him down.

ANTINOÖS   What's the meaning of this!

NOMAN stands in front of ANTINOÖS.

NOMAN   It's simple. We want our payment.   80

ANTINOÖS   You've had your payment.

NOMAN   It's not enough.

ANTINOÖS   It's all you're going to get.

NOMAN   I don't think so.

ANTINOÖS   How dare you . . . !

NOMAN   Pay up, then we'll go. If not, we'll stay, and take what we're owed.

ANTINOÖS   I'll throw you out myself!

ANTINOÖS goes to take hold of NOMAN. NOMAN grabs his hand, squeezes it. ANTINOÖS gasps in pain as NOMAN forces   90 him down to his knees

NOMAN   You think this woman here would want you for her husband? Eh? When you can't even stand up to a beggar like me?

ANTINOÖS is on his knees. NOMAN releases his grip and turns from him. He speaks to the other PLAYERS.

What do you think? Maybe she should take me for her husband.

PLAYERS cheer. NOMAN turns to PENELOPE.

Well, Lady? Would I suit? Could I play the part of a husband and a king?   10(

PENELOPE You could play it, no doubt, as well as you could play any other part.

NOMAN We're born to play any role we wish, and to wear any mask that fits.

The SUITORS are completely nonplussed and confused by this sudden turn of events. ANTINOÖS rises and turns to them.

ANTINOÖS Are we going to stand for this? Who does he think he is?

NOMAN I'm he who's been in the belly of the beast. I've descended to death's kingdom and risen again. I've survived all the   21(horrors heaven's sent against me. But now I'm home again, and I have weapons! Telemakhos! My bow!

TELEMAKHOS takes ODYSSEUS'S bow and quiver of arrows from his chair and throws them to NOMAN.

ANTINOÖS Treachery! You'll pay dearly for this, Telemakhos, after we've dealt with him . . .

NOMAN Your time of dealing's done. The doors are locked, and there's nowhere to go. This is the place where all journeys end.

ANTINOÖS Who are you?   23(

NOMAN   I'm the rag-man, the crow-man, the beggar at the door, and
                    you'd do well to fear me.

                    PLAYERS chant, as NOMAN strings the bow and fits an arrow.

PLAYERS   Beware the beggar at the door
                    The travelling man, tired and footsore
                    Who comes with marks of toil and war
                    Whose voice is like the lion's roar
                    Who'll skin your soul and leave it raw
                    And send it screaming down hell's maw
                    That stranger who's been here before   240
                    And wears Death's other face!

                    NOMAN takes off his mask, drops it to the floor.

NOMAN   The masks are off, the drama's done. I am Odysseus, and it's
                    time for all payments to be made.

                    *He draws the bow and aims it straight at ANTINOÖS. SUITORS
                    all cry out in fear and panic. PLAYERS grab hold of the
                    SUITORS.*

                    All freeze, in complete stillness.

                    *EUMAIOS, EURYKLEIA, TELEMAKHOS, and PENELOPE
                    narrate the slaughter of the SUITORS.*   250

EUMAIOS   Then he took the great bow and threw off his rags.

EURYKLEIA   Revealed in his splendour, the great king returned.

TELEMAKHOS   Unable to move all watched in horror.

PENELOPE   As he fitted an arrow and bent the bow double.

EUMAIOS   Found his first mark, and let swift death fly.

 maw *Throat.*

They continue their narrative, as ODYSSEUS, PLAYERS and SUITORS create a series of still, formal, stylised images, depicting the slaughter. Drumbeat accompanies this.

EURYKLEIA   The hall was filled with the sounds of slaughter.

TELEMAKHOS   Arrows flew thick and fast, each one found its mark.   260

PENELOPE   He struck them down where they stood.

EUMAIOS   Sent their souls to hell screaming.

EURYKLEIA   None found mercy, no man was spared.

TELEMAKHOS   All doomed that day to descend to the dark land.

PENELOPE   Falling to black death in blood and dust.

EUMAIOS   Until all were slain and the killing ended.

EURYKLEIA   And Odysseus stood triumphant among them.

TELEMAKHOS   Blood-caked, gore-matted, King Odysseus, lord of the island.

Drumbeat stops. All SUITORS now lie dead on the floor. ODYSSEUS turns to PENELOPE and TELEMAKHOS. There is a   **270** *pause, then PENELOPE walks up to ODYSSEUS.*

PENELOPE   Odysseus. My husband. Welcome home.

They embrace.

Some of the PLAYERS turn to speak to the audience. As they do, others take the bodies of the SUITORS offstage. EUMAIOS and EURYKLEIA leave, followed by TELEMAKHOS and PENELOPE. As each speaking PLAYER finishes their line, they also leave

1st PLAYER   Then the bodies were taken out and disposed of.

2nd PLAYER   The walls of the hall were washed of blood.

3rd PLAYER   The whole palace was cleansed and a feast was held.   280

4th PLAYER   There was music and song.

5th PLAYER   Laughter and rejoicing.

6th PLAYER	The whole island rang with the sound of celebration.
7th PLAYER	For Penelope had her husband.
8th PLAYER	Telemakhos had his father.
9th PLAYER	And Ithaka had its king.
10th PLAYER	And he ruled well and wisely for many years.

ODYSSEUS is now alone on stage.

The GODS enter, encircling ODYSSEUS.

HERA	Until . . .	290
APOLLO	At last . . .	
ATHENA	As had been foretold . . .	
POSEIDON	Death came from the sea to claim him . . .	
ZEUS	As it comes for all who live under the sun.	

The GHOST-FIGURE from scene 4 enters and stands on one side of ODYSSEUS. HERMES enters and stands on his other side.

GHOST-FIGURE	Noman.	
HERMES	His name.	
GHOST-FIGURE	Noman.	
HERMES	Your name.	300
GHOST-FIGURE	Noman.	

Death came from the sea to claim him *Nothing really is known about how Odysseus died. The mysterious prophecy* Death will come to you from the sea *was given to him in Tartarus by Tiresias. Some stories tell that Odysseus had a son by Circe, Telegonus, who, when grown, went seeking his father. Landing unannounced on Ithaka, Odysseus thought he was a pirate and went forth to repel him. The two met on the beach where Telegonus, unwittingly, killed the father he'd set out to find.*

The GHOST-FIGURE holds out its hand to ODYSSEUS.

ODYSSEUS   And it befits a man to meet with it bravely, and make that last journey outward, beyond the world's end.

Lights fade slowly to blackout.

The end.

DISCUSSION In this scene, you leave the world of magic and monsters, and return to the 'real' world of Ithaka.

Look at Noman's opening speech and discuss, as a class, how this speech tells you that you are back in the real world once more.

FREEZE-FRAME In groups, freeze-frame the moment when Noman reveals himself to be Odysseus. Aim to create a single, still image of dramatic power and tension. Try making this freeze-frame in a number of ways, until you've found the one that really works best.

Then, give each character in the freeze a line to say. This line might be a thought, or exclamation, a phrase or a single word. It should sum up what that particular character is thinking or feeling at that particular moment in time.

Finally, decide upon the best order in which these lines should be spoken, to achieve the best effect. Then present the freeze-frame to other groups, accompanied by the spoken lines.

DISCUSSION Looking at this scene, and the first scene discuss, in small groups, if you think Telemakhos knew about his father's plan from the beginning. If so, do you think there was anyone else that knew?

Support your opinions with examples from the text.

ARTWORK Imagine you're staging this scene for the theatre. Make a sketch of how you would like the closing moment to appear. Think about what effect you want this closing moment to have on the audience; it's the one they'll take with them when they leave.

In your sketch, show where all the characters onstage are standing, any props or pieces of scenery that might be there, and any special lighting you might want to use.

LOOKING BACK AT THE PLAY

1   DISCUSSION: THEMES

Apart from being a great adventure story, the *Odyssey* also deals with several important human themes. One is humankind's struggle against the forces of the world, and its attempts to control its own future: in other words, the struggle between free will and fate. In groups, go through the play, and find those moments that you feel deal most directly and openly with the struggle between fate and free will.

Then, using the sections you have found, discuss as a class what conclusion you think the playwright might have reached about free will and fate. Does he think fate or free will is stronger? Or has he left the question open?

2   ARTWORK: IMAGINING A FILM

There has been at least one film-version of the *Odyssey*. If you were making a film, what would your opening and closing shots be? Make two sketches, one showing the opening frame of your film and the other the closing frame. For each frame, write notes on what sounds the audience will be hearing, if you'll be using music, or voice-over narration, and what the camera will be doing, e.g. slow-fade in/out, close-up drawing back to long-shot. Think carefully about what opening and closing images of the story you'd want to give the audience.

3   ACTING

In groups, create a scene in which someone returns unexpectedly after a long absence. The drama of the scene should come from the surprise of the return, and the impact and effect it has on the characters. Discuss the whole thing beforehand, then work on and rehearse your scene several times up to a point where it could be performed, with skill, to an audience.

4   LANGUAGE

This dramatised version of the *Odyssey* uses a wide range of dramatic language: realistic dialogue, narrative (storytelling), monologue, choral speech, and verse. Find examples of these different language styles from the play and then discuss, as a class, why you think the playwright chose to use them when he did. Also discuss why you think the playwright did use this different number of language styles, instead of just using straightforward dialogue. What effect does the use of different styles have on the play, and the audience? What effect will it have on the actors?

5 MAPS: THE ANCIENT WORLD

Below is a map of the world as it was known in Odysseus's time. You can see where places such as Troy and Ithaka are marked. Trace out what you think might have been Odysseus's journey to Ithaka from Troy, marking down all the places, people and creatures he encounters in the play. Some of the places he visited are real: The Cattle of the Sun, for example, were kept on Sicily. But most of the other places are imaginary, although all would have been located within the world of the map.

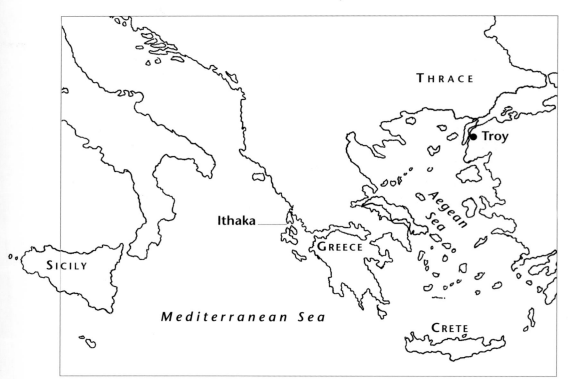

6   WRITING

As mentioned in one of the opening pieces, it is not really known how Odysseus died. All that Homer tells us in the *Odyssey* is that 'death will come to you from the sea'.

One possible death (Odysseus being killed unwittingly by his son, Telegonus) has been given elsewhere. Either:

a   write a scene for the theatre depicting Odysseus's death at the hands of Telegonus.

b   or write a short story, or poem, in which you invent a death for Odysseus.

For either of these pieces of work, draw upon what you have learned of Odysseus's character and the world he inhabits.

7   TRANSLATIONS

Since Homer first wrote his *Iliad* and *Odyssey* there have been numerous translations, and translations continue up to present time. It has been calculated that, since Medieval times, more copies of Homer's epics have been translated into English than any other single work. There have also been several excellent versions of the stories written especially for children and young people.

On page 80 there are three versions of the same scene – the storm that wrecks Odysseus's ship after his men have killed the Cattle of the Sun. Read these, then discuss, as a class or in groups, the differences and similarities between them, and which you prefer, and why.

In the first two, which are translations (one in prose, one in verse) it is Odysseus who is telling the story. In the third, which is a re-written version for young people, the story is told in the third person.

We lost the island and after it saw no more land, only sky and seas; but then the son of Cronos caused a lowering cloud to gather and stand over our hollow ship. Beneath it the deep turned thunder-dark. Nor did we scud much longer on our course: for suddenly a hurricane shrieked upon us from the West, ravening with mad gusts of wind, whose tearing violence carried away both our forestays. The mast toppled aft and all its gear ruined down into the waist; while the mast itself stretched backward across the poop and struck the helmsman over the head, smashing his skull to pulp. He dropped from his high platform in one headlong dive, and the brave spirit left his bones. Then Zeus thundered and at the same moment hurled a bolt of lightning upon the ship. Her timbers all shivered at the shock of the levin of Zeus. She filled with choking sulphur and brimstone smoke: her crew pitched out of her. For one instant they rode black upon the water, upborne like sea-fowl on the heaving waves past the black ship. Then the God ended their journey home.

(Translated by T.E. Lawrence (Lawrence of Arabia) and first published in 1932.
This edition published by Wordsworth Classics in 1992.)

But once we'd left the island in our wake –
no land at all in sight, nothing but sea and sky –
then Zeus the son of Cronus mounted a thunderhead
above our hollow ship and the deep went black beneath it.
Nor did the craft scud on much longer. All of a sudden
killer-squalls attacked us, screaming out of the west,
a murderous blast shearing the two forestays off
so the mast toppled backward, its running tackle spilling
into the bilge. The mast itself went crashing into the stern,
it struck the helmsman's head and crushed his skull to pulp
and down from his deck the man flipped like a diver –
his hardy life spirit left his bones behind.
Then, then in the same breath Zeus hit the craft
with a lightning-bolt and thunder. Round she spun,
reeling under the impact, filled with reeking brimstone,
shipmates pitching out of her, bobbing round like seahawks
swept along by the whitecaps past the trim black hull –
and the god cut short their journey home forever.

(Translated by Robert Fagles and published by Penguin in 1996.)

But as soon as they were out of sight of land, a great thundercloud came climbing up the sky until it overshadowed them with a black murk, though all around the sea was sunlit blue. Then a great squall of wind leapt upon them, tearing sails and rigging and snapping off the mast, which came crashing down striking the steersman on the head as it swept him overboard, so that he was dead before he hit the water. And from the dark heart of the stormcloud a jagged bolt of lightning whiplashed down and struck the ship, so that she staggered and reeled to the blow, filling with the stink of sulphur, and the men were flung overboard in a struggling mass.

For a while their heads bobbed like dark sea-birds on the waves. Then, one after another, they sank.

(From The Wanderings of Odysseus,
written by Rosemary Sutcliffe and published by Frances Lincoln in 1995.)

8 FINDING OUT

Using books, encylopaedias and CD Roms, see what you can find out about some of the following:

a The Greek Gods

b Other well-known Greek myths, such as:

Promtheus and the Creation of Man

Demeter and Persephone

The Twelve Labours of Herakles

Jason and the Quest for the Golden Fleece

Echo and Narcissus

Orpheus and Eurydice

There are, quite literally, hundreds more.

c Heinrich Schliemann, and his discovery of the 'real' Troy

9 ARTWORK

Design a theatre poster for a production of this play. Think carefully about what image you want to take from the play to create the poster.

8 READING – OTHER ODYSSEYS

The word 'odyssey' has now come to mean a long and arduous journey, into the unknown, in search of something precious. Since Homer wrote his *Odyssey* there have been many more such 'journey' or 'quest' stories written, and made into films. Some are myths and folk tales from different parts of the world, such as *The Voyages of Sindbad the Sailor*. Some are realistic novels, such as *The Grapes of Wrath*, written by the American novelist John Steinbeck in the 1930s and some are science fiction films such as Stanley Kubrick's *2001: A Space Odyssey*, made in 1969. The Irish writer James Joyce also wrote a very famous novel called *Ulysses*, published in 1922, which re-located the *Odyssey* to Dublin, where a man called Leopold Bloom wanders around the city from dawn till night on 6th June, 1904.

See how many other 'odyssey' stories you can think of or find: they might be books, plays, television dramas, or films.

Finally, the *Odyssey* has also inspired many poets. Here's an extract from one written by the English poet, Alfred, Lord Tennyson, in 1832. It describes an imagined, final voyage by Ulysses (the Roman version of 'Odysseus').

Come, my friends,
'Tis not too late to seek a newer world.
Push off, and sitting well in order smite
The sounding furrows; for my purpose holds
To sail beyond the sunset, and the baths
Of all the western stars, until I die.
It may be that the gulfs will wash us down:
It may be we shall touch the Happy Isles,
And see the great Achilles, whom we knew.
Tho' much is taken, much abides, and tho'
We are not now that strength which in old days
Moved earth and heaven; that which we are, we are;
One equal temper of heroic hearts,
Made weak by time and fate, but strong in will
To strive, to seek, to find, and not to yield.